The Fire
Enlightening

February 20th, 2019

a collection of poetry by

Garret C. Tufte

Spartan Press

Kansas City, Missouri

spartanpresskc.com

Spartan
Press

copyright 2018 Garret C. Tufte

www.tuftesvariations.com/

first edition: 11 7 5 3 2 1

ISBN: 978-1-946642-53-0

LCCN: 2018943839

Layout: Jeanette Powers

Cover Design: Garret C. Tufte

This project was made possible, in part, by generous support
from the Osage Arts Community. Osage Arts Community
provides temporary time, space and support for the creation of
new artistic works in a retreat format, serving creative people
of all kinds — visual artists, composers, poets, fiction and
nonfiction writers. Located on a 152-acre farm in an isolated
rural mountainside setting in Central Missouri and bordered by
¾ of a mile of the Gasconade River, OAC provides residencies to
those working alone, as well as welcoming collaborative teams,
offering living space and workspace in a country environment
to emerging and mid-career artists. For more information, visit
www.osageac.org

Author's Note:

This book is dedicated to all of my friends and family, whose saintly patience and support has made it possible; to the poets of Northeast Kansas for creating an incredible community, and the many venues that provided the stage from which this writing has sprung forth; much thanks goes to Spartan Press for their publishing bravado; and of course, endless appreciation goes to the indomitable Jeanette Powers for her tireless efforts to accommodate my requests.

My hope is that you, dear reader, with the path expressed within, may find your own spark of fire or lightning, that you shall know both common and unique truths, and that you may revel in this world with integrity, compassion, dignity, justice, love, and all virtue, spiced with some level of rascality and a healthy grain of salt.

Toward that end, this book contains the following material that people have been known to object to: Strong language, stronger rhetoric, sexual language, drug and alcohol use, some minor violence, and critical political thought.

Table of Contents

An Arrogant Destiny   9

Hammurabi's Blitz   10

The "We" Seed   12

Reparation Fixation   14

A Response to a Lack of Colour   16

Pit Stop on the Way to the Grand Canyon   18

Escape From the Land of Dreams,   21
   or Lighting Fire in a New World

A Frog Sees the Lightning   33

A Reprieve   50

The Sum of All Parts   55

Arrogant Destiny

I don't know you know what's going on here.
That I am your man, your plan,
hero doing all he can.

So much I do with the freedom
to build, make, write, and create without tedium.
A good woman by my side,
and you'll think I was born of the Gods to grant all.
To make the world a paradise,
with all man and woman ensured.
To make it last in touch with nature,
harmonious and beautiful beyond compare,
with love and comfort free to all,
energy unlimited, life always now.

Without war nor hate
nor twisted collective fate.
Free and yet conjoined,
humanity organically
spreading at a reasonable rate.
The homeworld alive and bountiful, free,
and containing actual privacy.

I don't know you know what's going on here.
You're at the center of it, megalomaniacally.
How can you stand by and watch this happen to me?
Forced into an arrogant destiny.

Hammurabi's Blitz

So, if one were to step to this
I'd respond right quick
a little finger's worth your stake
of this immense stati-wake.

Ultimately there's no touching me,
you fool who coos, you lose
the test of time you cannot see
it's beyond your mental capacity.

Set in stone, a masterpiece, Hammurabi's
code's in infancy
blitz to find it, took the new way,
not blinded.

Serving up lovely sweet buds, I'll
wrestle the HUD out your blood, crack it
with a splitting sound and cannibalize
the better attributes, cuz I'm seeing
automatons better spent around gravitons,
hanging loose near center of gravity,
acting all tough bitch but got no
pull to go with it.

If you hit the rock, it's coming with a shock,
your bones are weak to this incredible feat
unstoppable leet speak, both prose and

poetic, never failing, game-changing,
no equivalent to this classical and
contemporary lyricist, physicist, economist-
ic, artistic, mage-like, sage-like, saint
Christopher hold on tight;
sailing, wailing, assailing, force with no recourse.

/ Son /

Imbibing, incising, inciting, and
describing.

Your greatest wish and implementing it.
That's Hammurabi's Blitz.

The "WE" Seed

So it seems being divine,
demanding of steel,
demanding of oil,
demanding of scores of resource material,
demand of your craft,
demands little of another.
Rather stands beside each other.

The "WE" seed, plant in spring or summer.

Feeling, reeling, from attraction, attention
loneliness away, very much slain
no more distance, no longer alone
you mayday lady, came to the scene,
checked the patient for life, and found he not bleeding,
but coursing a rushing river.

He rides it as whitewater
cruising along with the current.
He scoops up buckets, slakes his thirst
the fruit of hanging trees, regenerated sustenance.

The canoe has room for two.
Think what we could do!

I care not our ages, our differences,
you are divine beauty, and more,
you are to be loved, it's unjust otherwise,

you queen of the night and day, you outshine
the sun and moon combined.

You are the brightest flame, the spark.
You could melt stone, burn white
your radiance about crossing arcs.

You beautiful, brilliant divine.

Reparation Fixation

Twist a knob
to power 'ON'.

Spin a wheel
to charge the field.

Press any key
to boot from CD.

Flash instruction
on electronic conduction.

Shifting space for partitions
like crop rotations.

Slash and burn technique,
rewrite the field of wheat.

                              Seeds to stalk instantaneously.

Wind-blown seeds from the neighbor's field
sprout stringy and fibrous, reducing my yield.

These vines and brambles sap their energy.
A never-ending task, cutting free with machete.

As I tend to one plot,
my focus away from the money crop,

The neighbor's got it in his head,
that his weeds make it his homestead.

I return to find no cloudberry bushes,
but a rock wall with no entrances.

It seems the person to whom it is attributed,
cared not to his fruit, for it withered.

But rather, lacking any other purpose,
appropriated what was free to begin with.

Machiavelli said, "Being unarmed causes one to be despised",
so an open range attracts slavers to enclose and privatize.

Now nothing grows and the fields lay fallow,
because to plant again is to till all plots.

But one conspicuous structure takes up the lot,
imprisoned is that miraculous fruit I had wrought.

So a final question I pose to thee; how to use one's energy:

Better to beat on the wall till a crack,
and gain my previous crop back;

or to start anew with what I know
to be better seeds to sprout and grow?

But the answer from you I needed not beckon,
because the truth, now and forever, is the second.

A Response to a Lack of Color

I see hexagonal cylinders,
web work composed by arachnid builders.

Mitochondrial geodesic domes,
frosted corners of symmetrical cones,
latticework and scaffolding invented,
each unit grown the rate of nanometer per photon intake.

Trajectory curvatures from gross weight
slingshots about orbs in open space. A sphere's efficient shape
twists and tumbles, a pace we cannot relate.

Parallel lines and horizontal extensions do not meet
spiral circumference, calculated error, statistical defeat.
Additional dimensions create possibility, not absolutely.

Skies of blue: refraction of light omits a spectrum Earth
cannot see, its residents vicariously.

Clouds of white: strands of wisps absorbing
threads and strings and blue pearls man o' war
drifting tentacles pulsing waves shorn condensing fall,
slide marbles till terminal curves flatten tails,
drop to pools of waves expanding, flowing
over obstruction reversing destructive interference.

Trees of green: roots of scales and branching tubers

converging to vaster arteries sucked
to inversion open air, extending out fractal
imperfect dance to individual nuanced patterns of
stereotyped veined formations, living and dying the breath
of consistent astronomical intent.

Babies cry: they loose electric signals, freshly
paved pathways of sensory perception,
imagination influx articulating fearful instance.

A world: growing outward ever more stacked
shells of interlaced generations, building above and atop
dying systems organic, artificial, and abstract.

Paper avalanches submerge spelunking adventurers
mining golden words, baskets of ink-stained
scrolls discovered under mountains discarded,
significant, but not whole-hearted.

A thankless mission wading through dreck for
permission to find a paid position in interconnected
machinery-bloated frustration.
An oxygenated continuum ever regenerating, but grease drying
with asymptotic declination.

Roses look red, violets look blue,
tulips look yellow occasionally,
bees look striped, some tigers look white,
but cardboard is corrugated,
because reason is truth
and colors are debated.

Pit Stop on the Way to the Grand Canyon

For what be the reasons that there be only one season?

A single lesson continues on
with little concern for the daily rite, nor wrong.

This is a journey stuck in mid-session,
short of the Grand Canyon.

A family on their way to this destination had parked their car at a gas station. There's a little diner and a jukebox, there's a pretty waitress working 'round the clock. The family had been there so long they'd already gone through four waitresses strong.

"Won't it be incredible!" said little Suzy to her brother Everly.

Everly didn't look away from his ever-present, distracting gameplay. "I know it will be, because it already is. And before it's ever rotten, we'll long be dead and forgotten."

The father Henry chimed in at the first word of nihilistic sin. "There's no beating nature's inevitabilities, and bemoaning your lack of capability only instigates your own calamity."

Everly never responded easily, for his mind remained in fantasy. Infinite reality was ignored, for fictional wandering of limited scope but immediate reward.

Little Suzy tried again vainly, this time with her mother Maggie, "Won't it be lovely, Mommy, to see such majesty?"

Her mother was taken aback by the attempt at her comment. Her gaze had been flitting between the eyes of each visitor upon sitting. A protective mood arranged her thoughts, never betrayed to any crafty lots. "Oh yes, but only if you wear that blouse up higher. I am a keen scryer; there is no escape from the briars of the liar. Were he to see your chest bent down, I fear the terrible scream you would sound. Stay close, and be satisfied; curiosity and ambition are undignified. And besides, who could stand all those prying eyes?"

Little Suzy craned her neck and scanned the section to her left. They gambled and cursed and shared stories in verse. Whole groups joined in the chorus, and with it there was much ruckus.

"Scared true; they've been here longer than us," said Henry, keeping an eye on his daughter's curiosity.

Suzy leaned closer, and whispered softly, "What a motley bunch! They must have seen the canyon before getting lunch! It can only make sense to have such confidence!"

Suzy and Henry puzzled over the colorful lot, discerning two prominent figures in spots.

One had golden hair, a prominent crown, a strong upper body, but was always sitting down. He carried a scepter of incredible gold, marble, and luster. Sculpted from the finest material, over a thousand years, with a touch of the spiritual. He moved ever so slowly, and only spoke to his admirers disinterestedly.

One other rose above the rank, deftly maneuvering swift, never to sink. Bounding to and fro with such speed, more than this one could not read. So quick he moved, to be without shape, even the best could hardly catch his wake. As soon as one spied his formless hide, another joker appeared, lived, laughed, loved, and died. He lifted the glasses of his admirers, stroked their beards, and diluted their vernaculars. None knew of his presence about; only those who could live without.

And so they stared intently upon these creatures about the yon, giving each the proper respect to know that, at least, they inspired the rest. For little was known of the Canyon as yet, but from the action of those two gents.

(I believe it wise here, within this tale, to tell another, erstwhile the first shall fail. Another gentleman within the diner, heard tell of the two characters over the fire. Much lauded were their adventures, so much that he ventured, out upon the blistering sands, past rocking-horse, lizard, and man, to find the abode from which they spoke, and know their characters firsthand. He was ever active yet scholarly, born with equal affinity of mind, spirit, and body. The seeming immortal war of the two bands was beyond the scope of any man, but he reasoned much justice still, with what little he could understand. So he journeyed onward toward this abode when, by accident alone, along the Canyon itself, he strode! But too distracted was he for such infinity; he placed a higher value upon divinity. The battle of the characters he must seek. For how else could he instruct the meek?)

While Maggie was busy protecting the family, and Everly was invested in another egotistical fantasy, and Henry pondered the devilish characters' persuasive ingenuity, Little Suzy could feel the pressure building steadily. She wanted to know ever so much, and the pain of waiting was becoming a crush. What ever could she do if not a one of the family would take her to view? The Canyon was just over the hill, but this her pleading could not fulfill. She waved down her waitress, that wondrous woman coming with gifts, and asked for just a pinch. When she returned with some paper, Little Suzy was a ready creator. This time, with her favorite brown crayon, Little Suzy would draw the Grand Canyon.

Escape from the Land of Dreams;
or Lighting Fire in a New World - In Five Parts

Part I:

Absolute, you do
utmost, of course
rewards your chores
cleans the floors.

More doors beyond static wars
deceptive reception, explanation obsolescence
consolidated effervescence
due more, indebted lessons.

Youth source, storm course
expressing vivisection, dissecting the abstract intravenous
fountain success
reanimating momentum, invitational deference continuum.

Goals extol, vitriol
twin visage, explicit spirit
effects access to it.

Reverend asked you to submit habit, rabbit, just frantic static, prophetic eclectic, composite of logical intentional action-in-preparation, verifying and complying and pressing, on against divested interests foment cool, accepting divergence.

Part II:

The question of politics, answered with a mirror.

The mirror will give or deny on attitude alone.

A step a year by you seems little,
but look to your left and right, and
take the hand of another,
and your solitary walk becomes a marching armada.

The debate is over.
Fruits come through progress toward brighter future.
What can you do?
Rock on, walk on, my friends.
Rock and roll, walk and extol and
beat on the wall till a crack.
Take your future BACK.

I don't know you,
not where you're from or your personal habit.
But I know you want.
Sometimes hard to see
through miasma of abstract bleeding greed.
I see all drink it freely,
first come first thirst, but
vampires do not give birth.
Sure, eternal life would be nice, but
wooden stakes and pitchforks through castle walls slice.

America's entitled, not to the good life,
means little to most,
sheltered and clothed since birth,
rather, elevated attitude,
a position above
to look down and judge.
Opinionated minutiae cause collective grin,
for the win.
The general ordered by the drill sergeant,
twisted to fight in the trenches.
Absurd the fight obvious,
over a no man's land not worth the losses, and
nonsensical debates rage between sides split on the causes.
You waste your breath
for our entertainment.

All legitimacy disregarded, and
justice flattered for cheeky dimples on a forced smile,
above a torso dead and bloated.
Frankenstein's wizardry used against better judgment,
square pegs in round holes.
The normal force reverses course,
and the catastrophic event
eventuates, but
instead of prepare,
we play games of truth or dare,
where trust is divided,
the dare is derided,
the act on display debated,
opinionated voyeurism's time wasted.

resources depleted with steady hands,
the brand says;
get your aggression out on that punching bag,
ignore the man behind the curtain,
it's certain,
youth's anger's root is this perversion.

He'll tell you,
and bribe you,
put you in the iron maiden,
cause your derision.
He knows your inner workings,
he's seen brain scannings,
and psychological manipulation
inter-socially,
easy to see,
practiced since the 50's.

He's such a taste for it,
he'll make you want it, this psychological abuse,
but soon as you use a piece, he'll use the whole pie against you.
Soon as you know yourself, he'll have known you sooner.
We're predictable, you see, on the whole, endlessly.
Sorry to break it to you, but the more you know,
the less of you
the man can screw.

But better yet, take a tip from me;
see, the system's predictable deductively,
human action and opinion act inductively;

meaning, we're cornered into "percentage-likely".
But the system's mechanisms operate with certainty.

The machine is restricted logically,
but there is no limit to human potentiality.

Part III:

Weaker words disappear
behind a quakening wave,
they point in the direction we crave
an equilibrium, that adamantium-like state,
"to be a rock and not to roll",
"hang on to yourself,"
your health, and your soul.

I'm dropping all pretense,
demolishing the fence,
an obstacle waiting
for the end of its heyday.
Stand and deliver
your best measure!

Where have we, indeed, been?

Through protozoic past,
depth of history deeper than any abyss,
the very definition and the truth of man,

beginning defined, a line,
some date at which inclined.
And after, as stories begun,
we sing, we sung, historical leverage,
we find increased message, as we read and write,
the good tidings
find their way on screen,
they come together and with intent,
laid out before all to see,
independent of geography.

Freedom from is more negative,
that freedom to, by extension,
is independent toward some score.
What handicap? More a reminder.

On through history,
empires to kings,
onward crossed freedom's crest,
rode that ever-wave on,
flung Caesars off towers,
dropped kings from cliff hangings,
we took our people's birth writings.
Always stayed within history;
when you, they gave a redder day,
you, me, we, made always.
Defining systems and social compacts,
Political and abstract.

Part III - Part "B":

Wheels lead at speeds
akin to their leanings,
curving with force directional.

Skidding along railings.

What laws unchangeable?
Scraping the grindstone railing,
and repeating,
degrading its state.

Such that, the path you make,
outside imposed lines,
pushes forth, through barriers,
you rail skaters.

Grind to the bone.
Grind to the bone.
Grind to the bone.
Grind to the bone!

But I digress,
you good folks amassed,
we've important business at hand.

Much to be said,
subsequently read.
Making bread?

Swords onward to plowshares,
another volunteer a day,
life gained / time planting.

Much more to be said here,
but we continue toward
the event of seers,
the land of dreamers.
Ascend a height never imaginable,
grand vistas and stark visage.
Ride the wind!
You won't regret it.

Past decades influence better grades,
experience gained where highest stake,
we've bet on our progress,
an accelerating mess.

But wound spool renewal,
ouroboros triple cylindrical,
spatial dimensional rotations.
Now try the 'T':
temporal twister,
time turner,
single directional flow,
knowledge offering to
mitigate and mitigate away
the irrational opinionated enclaves.

Between competing forces we lie, a sty,

chaotic / ordered,
by extension our forces,
our best approximation of the divisive powers,
simply explained to all who keep their eyes arrayed.

Dropping all pretense as insistence,
returning to the point,
the point of focus,
bounced back to, and now onward,
toward ever-resurgence.

Part IV:

Cleaning out the past is a long dance,
longer still with every regret made in the present.

The future's a *now*, shifting,
stacking broken floors atop crumbling ceiling.

Paying for a past regenerating
with scientifically-weaponized spirit engineering.

Past mistakes awake a monster
feeding on what is now slaughter,
presently-known improper imposter.

The shape of things to come:
floating cities lifted by cloud formations,

height no object,
made from energy wasted daily,
our daily drive toward disaccord;
making what future we take, and bake, to create;
to save truly limited, valuable resource;
spent to no good end, shitty trend,
better left to storage sheds.

The shape of things to come:
our understanding's taking a pounding;
we'll be flippin' our shit,
if you know it, "fortunate
son", you better see the light in front of thee,
that shines a golden birth of beautiful new earth,
like paradise, it cries your wandering eyes,
it cries, "those eyes cry every night for you",
a morrow lies beyond your wandering eyes.

We will live to see the city,
repeat after me,
we will live to see the city.

Part V:

No need to pity.

Little by little our future, lo and behold,
just like a hundred years ago,

you see, our collective energy, creativity,
operates slower than we relate.
We perceive consumable dreams,
and think we've seen all that can be.
The end of history?
All's been done only if you think extra-temporally.

But that is not today, and it is not tomorrow.
That thought's better reserved escaping sorrow.
But when velocity reached, jettison restrictive weights, and
meet the vacuum of space without hamstrings.

You dreamers, always pushing the boundaries,
expanding the surroundings,
prepping troops to explore uncharted territories.
The time is now to end your fictional wanderings,
pack your saddle bags,
ride the rising tide to lands
only seen in mind.
And don't just take my word for it,
there is historical precedent.
"Everything has been invented already,"
to paraphrase a quote from 1890.
Advancement-capable in every single category.
But we lack willful responsibility.
Better to leave difficulties to corporate entities
and governmental agencies,
of course they have our best interests at heart,
forty years of reduced purchasing power with longer hours,
chipping away every advance we make,

wrangling us into pens
made of emperor's invisible gates.

The end?

It does not need to be this way.

The shape of things to come:
inverting a pyramid represents transference.
Only question is how bloody a revolt hence:
dog and pony trampling calamity to finality,
or honest institution, with trouble only temporary.

The longer we wait,
the less a choice
it will be.

A Frog Sees the Lightning

From frog to foot to frog to foot...

A 50 ton leather-sole stomps about
the giant slips of Liberty's sandal.
Watch out frog! Don't block the footfalls.

"Who said that?"

Don't do like the mouse, and you're free to roam around.
Get all the flies and spiders that you like.

"Where are we going this time?" asks the inquisitive one.

Bah, such questions...
The questions best action abide
a horse of course, dressed in silver,
a goddess above flying
dipping wings, dripping rain,
floating about, showers alloyed blades, implement ready,
see them strike, as earth meets sky, sky meets earth,
these astral-biological wonders, fallen in love, their charges
parallel induced touched at a canyon crossed over arcs,
fly sparks, reels wooden earth, sways at wind and storm, forces
primal, earth and sky connecting, liquids, gases,
solidifying time tests, interweaving atmospherics.

"What did that thing say?"

"I don't know man, it and them others you seen them too, is like, stomping along, you gotta watch out of course, see little tadpole, I know you just came out of the water, and this here's the land, and you got them things all around, they don't bother much or may some if you're not careful, best to stay away, they might reach down and grab ya, I heard stories, and those four legged ones are to really worry about, they're all round and will gobble you right up."

"What is this place?"

"Tonga-tinga-mondo-lingo-riva-piva-cana-widget."

"The what?"

Name's not the game.

"What?"

***

Hey, hey you.

"Frogs and silver trees and giants and four-legged beasties, slithering snakes, bears all furry-"

"What's that?"

"You just interrupted."

"Me? I was asking if this was all real, like, for fucking real?"

... [awkward pause]

"So-"

"Yeah."

"So the-"

"Yeah."

"But wha-"

"Yeah."

"Alright."

... [less awkward pause]

"So what's there to eat?"

"Well, the little scampering things see, they're crunchy and tasty, and they're all over the place. And when the rains come, see, they come out all the more. Watch for that.

"Rains?"

"Yep, water falls from the sky."

"Really? No way!"

"Yup. Look, it's starting." Boom, boom. Giant globs of water

hit the ground about, with tremendous crashes, splashing
everything. The frogs hop toward shelter, a large cavern with
a smooth, hard floor. They watch the huge drops crash outside
the entrance. A deep, rumbling voice comes from within...

Ah, the rains come with new presents!
Gifts from the sky, gifts from our gods.
Few they come when faith falls victim to wicked persuasion,
propped up, standing with rationalizations,
as a child, cries why,
that bauble be mine!

What of my child?
What does he want, for whom does he cry?
For loved onces, gave birth,
met newborn face with loving eyes.
That child cries, for wants and pines.

Now who he to know the greater?
As much true personal,
but gain with years,
gain sight of seers,
then deny, O deny!
Why for self's sake deny wants,
though cries issue forth, but not for he,
loneliness be minor feat.
Experience gained, to know the temporary,
while permanence falls heavy,
heavy on the soul,
watching gifts drop,

drench the witness in acknowledgment,
sacrament, thankfulness.
And worry etches the brow,
impossible not allow,
scripts and fleeting life snippets
pass by worried eyes,
wandering toward a greater score.
Fie the battle!
Victory worth less,
when loser be blessed.
God bless us!
Yes, he did!
Again and again,
with fervor,
with paradise and free will assured,
us creatures grown up from the earth,
gifted with a light of sorts,
one we can hardly understand,
blinding too,
averting our eyes toward faux value,
and virtue in innocence lost!
O cry out for day, cry out for the natural way!
But what return entail,
suffer in roundabout journey,
building artifice,
our very nature challenged.
Have we worth it?
Have we worth what?
The denatured synthetic future,
scores living,

billions surviving,
worth the synthesis,
technological and human progress,
or a blasted, wasted paradise readies its fruits,
withered and struggling to survive.
Cries for the return!
Be you human?
Then fly you fools toward the future vast!
A paradise cries for your wandering eyes!
Return not, but look forward, up,
grasp and strive with each aching bone,
for that future world!
Strain with your back, legs, sinews,
beyond which your heart would burst,
let it burst!
Cough and stagger through,
though your chains be holding you,
be attached not to rock,
but your fellow!
If bonded forever they be,
as they or we seem,
know the chains bind all, equally.

Night and day break above our heads,
our souls long to be free of this night,
this shadow casting pall.
Staged as a tragedy for all,
meant for failure, we?
Let that be!
Give your truth stage,

that truth of staging,
the setting by which you live,
we live out another day.
Strain those chains and break that staging!
This world, our Earth, cares less for us daily.
Speaking in harsh tones,
harsher the more rebellious the child,
her children, her best progeny,
her most gifted sons and daughters.
Throw those shackles and hear her voice,
do right by hook or by crook.
She will cast us off without a thought,
patience waning with every drill cut.
There is no shame, her voice, in following
it gains in pitch and urgency.
What voices drown her out?
Senses of duty and responsibility,
interpersonal morality,
to continue paying debts accrued wrongly.
For the health,
not of only of yourself,
but some sense of humanity,
shared collective fate demands,
spurred by her warning,
a humanist accepts responsibility for progressing.
The gate will not fit the chains binding humanity.

"Did you hear that? It's like a low rumbling."
That's how sky mated with earth.
As the shifting shells in interlace

as god of sky and god of earth felt their spring,
when they met, when they do meet, how so?
See the lightning.
Watch the earth and sky
tremble in rapturous ecstasy.
They crash into and within deepest charge,
us mortals stand and observe,
they procreate divine and sublime
ancient and prescient meaning,
a primitive birthing,
they meet, met, will ever interact,
tearing the physical fabric
between their connect.
Yes, feel the moment,
it's primal and vital to your and our health,
a grand interweaving,
vast expanse of gods beyond men and women,
vapor chops the sky,
states of matter materialize,
in front of our eyes,
this great act of intercourse, and while
swirling, curling, enraptured feeling,
tremble in anticipation at
our world in the act of procreation.

Could you see that as act?
Special we be... indeed.
Strings and wisps threading fogs and flows
'tween stones, about birds' wings,
as flitting as an evening,

with peace, serenity, and harmony,
the major tendency,
shocking moments temporary,
like material meant to stay that way
conditionally circumstantial level
depending on the environmental,
temperature and gravity vary wildly,
depend spatially,
distance to and from other bodies,
alteration by means of transportation,
vicinity,
while forces called wild be often consistent,
a paradox of perception,
self-observation and consciousness,
awareness,
bridging harmonies over long-expanses,
complexity from simplicity,
scaled-in to the level of human,
ourselves interactive masses,
grown of building blocks,
given capabilities,
calamitous often,
stranger than our animal brethren.
Yes, we are the effect.

How great a cause?
As great and grand the universe itself,
in all glory, it, we, are the progeny of history,
an apex, daily spending our precious fits.
And who could say as much?

Who could be the one
or two or three or more
to scream to the heavens,
when God hears for sure,
but our fellow man's warped to the core.

For this man,
the question's no mystery
whether God hears our pleas,
it indeed does,
and answers come,
though vague and strange,
satisfactory.
Asked by some,
why would God allow such a thing?
God allows all.
We are free,
a great gift (another for those counting).
Direct action beside a rule.
More difficult among "Gods and Men,"
that of man, of humankind,
the church upon this earth,
us stewards of planet and fellow.
Does God hear you? Of course.
Does Man hear you? No? Make it so.
Search long enough,
and answers come.
Answers, yes. Great!
Now we know, correct?
Right and good, eh?

No? The answer is a bitch,
but not God's realm,
for Nature determines action.
Have you noticed? She calls...

"Where's it going now?"

*"Every couple hours it walks away
for a few minutes into the other room. I don't know."*

... [Frog No. 1 pees on the floor. The man returns.]

Nature calls her children to action,
a biological imperative.
And here come simple answers, yes.
Physical interactions,
energy dependency,
cells upon cells upon cells,
flowing through and within each other,
sending our messengers,
dividing, breeding, so quietly,
in tandem, a ballet.
Yes, the story continues,
nature bursts through obstacles.
"Human nature," they say,
is our downfall, eh?
Our actions, more or less set,
predetermined by necessity.
That is nature calling.
What of civility?

Tempering and honing the calling,
actions deliberate "enlightenment,"
touching clouds of heaven.
The sky flows through all open space.
Until, or unless,
we breach other spheres,
beyond our comfortable nature,
an abyss stretches out endlessly,
before our very noses.
Planets, other "gods"
with their own temperament
call or scream away,
as Venus does,
screaming in agony,
boiling away, relatively,
as us wolves upon porcupine,
without underbelly,
no soft patch
or succulence or gentleness.
Anathema to our nature.
They say devils and demons live there.
Nonetheless a state,
peculiar to us or perhaps the crow,
that spreads to areas without water,
never too hot nor too cold, to make another home.

So much, done in the past,
questioning not the consequence.
And now, we see them about,
and answers so well known, available to all.

Yet divisive distraction
denies our nature,
denies the enlightened.
Racing to the end.
The faster race,
the quicker finish.
Slow and low, extends competition.
If anyone hopes to make it,
to grasp our nature and future,
accept limitation,
but fulfill potential.
Our goals, what are they even?
You tell me what you think?!

... [He yells through the open door.]

Don't care to answer?
Then listen!
A healthy long life for you, me,
your children and grandchildren!
This is how we do that.

... [He takes a clipboard, a pair of charts, and a white board.]

Equalize intake, output,
energy parity, infrastructure,
intend to ends here, here and here.
This mechanism limits waste.
Distribute goods and services this way.
Efficiency counts, and see how so.

Even if it takes more work,
the direct plan is preferred.
Value determined this way.

In all great projects,
you need the help of many.
Even the very powerful,
when they get on board,
would still make a struggle.
We are fighting against deep-seated interests
that don't translate to individual intent.
There are parts of our brains that
will disagree conceptually.
Loosing control is hard to imagine,
more so the longer it took,
to come to fruition.
How must that feel?

A castle so strenuously constructed,
strong enough to last eons,
upon ramparts you stand and gaze,
the sun vibrant before you,
a victor of a grand battle,
owing none to another,
to sit upon a throne,
one's own.

Now that castle shakes,
it quakes, by your own making.
But do not despair!

Do not stir at the rumblings about,
the change and the wild.
These forces breed in due time,
and bring forth beautiful progeny.
Living for your betterment, no matter who you be,
nor what station nor color nor creed:
The power behind enlightened nature's calling.
She calls to you.
While the heavens dance about her,
through and between all crevasses.
Watch the lightning, earth and sky mate,
as nature piques enlightenment,
as dipoles bridge connection,
as the opposed nonetheless embrace.
The myriad wonder, that once upon a time and place,
gave birth to life flowing through our veins,
the bridge of chaos and order,
the syntheses of dream and reality,
the wild and the civilized,
the left and the right,
nature and God in one being,
the quantum and the macro,
humanity in between,
the sudden impact,
the deliberate act,
the fractal dance,
splitting hairs without care,
and caring not for split hairs,
emerge a greater pattern.
And these our children!

They shall spread across all whose good soul they touch.
"Humanity lies between competing forces,"
and our charge to mediate, to allow transition,
stepping free of interaction,
lightning rods at appropriate location,
aiding, abetting, abiding connection
amongst friends and family,
nature and society,
even round the globe,
infinitely loosing
cupids arrows upon hearts of stone,
warming hearths and homes,
rewarding happiness,
want and need.
You see!
When you hear these words,
you see.
This is no mere dream.
It can be reality! Matters of time and pressure, only.

... [He turns away from the door.]

Rest it upon me to say such things?
That if necessary "A,"
then fucking "A"!
Classic tropes,
reluctant heroes spin heads so,
reluctant villains too.
Who's to say?
That once God willed angels

destructive flames
lay ignorance to waste,
too brutal enlightenment,
wisdom held sway,
but what wisdom that destroy?
God relegated to the classic world,
long passed,
what wisdom in past fades
as waves shear the cliff face.
Wisdom, yes, but that of yesterday!
O compassion, still,
grip my soul tightly, O gift!
Tend your tree and let not wither,
for vengeance's sword glitters,
greater with the morning light.
Yes, the sun will soon rise.
What will become of the day?
Striving forces of enlightened nature,
contemplation complete,
dreams finished, and the day awaits.

This hand stirs with new dawn's breath.
See it lift, see it rise.
Be it palm... or fist...

A frog sees the lightning.

A Reprieve

The dazzling light blinds
these receptors, fried.
People and all worldly objective measure
strain the brain, heavy motions
emote with blinders.

Fie impatience and satisfaction
the message flipped for release,
purposes getting it out early,
that least ruin brought on,
this man or woman, whoever
the recipient be. Messages in
the bottle of emotion, release
when time tests snap.

This is hard, choosing between
a feeling and intention, sudden
volcanic bursts, rumblings in the earth
gave warning, seen it coming, chomping
at the bit, rearing to go, to fight.
But what enemy? The action is spastic,
constant, and yet predictably mechanistic,
this diplomatic mental dam breaches waters,
flow constrained many days, waters rise, wind
rushes, competing voices play for attention, and
I want you, but also me.

Best defense, a good offense? No battle evident, yet
something is missing it's better half. A reprieve.
Outer and inner directional warping awareness, catching
some sense slowly slaking thirst, feasting on reality
the interior and exterior, equal substance, existence
defined by some line at which inclined, pushing the scrimmage
forward, up, out, and away, quarterback taking deeper snaps,
dodging defenders, scoring in a game if worth playing. Living
for the hail Mary, that miraculous highest of the high.

And we find a great, long history of screwing oneself over.
Now I am not the only one to see the horror of other's actions
deplorable, nonetheless taken.

This observer wonders what mirror
abides, how man or woman in such states carry forth through
quagmire, dancing with devils, fighting the beast,
twisting message through continued action.
The struggle against imaginary enemies, is abstract.
And much maligned art reflects life, thought, emotion,
first, second, and third person.

Dashing paint indiscriminately, dousing with chaos, ordered in
retrospect, history written by the victor,
and the art of life splattered, making heads and tails
of the nonsense. A random neuron fired a round friendly,
seeking breaks that need patching, straightening truth,
even in the least deserving place, a place whether evoking,
responsive to touch, responsive to word and deed. Skills spoiled
on druthers, except listening.

Take, absorb, understand, pattern,
make sense, deliberate strange, release.
Done. No turning back.

Anew, seeking a reprieve, from something given,
now something received. Pendulum swings,
and love hurts both ways. Still, yet,
a solemn and calm flame burns warm and soothing waves
across this body and mind. Alight anew with
day's dawning, with all longing, and loving.

The only direction left.

The Sum
of All Parts

a play for the stage by

Garret C. Tufte

Part I:

"A Gathering at Jack's Den"

Part II:

"Synergy in the Key of Swing"

Part III:

"21st Century X New Roman"

Cast of Characters:

Tonya Seneca:	A young, able academic.
Saltpeter Faulk:	A wizened bartender.
Seth W. Markowitz:	A satirist and art critic.
Clarence R. Fringe:	A practical joker.
Alexander D. Cellini:	A revolutionary.
Madonna Della Verita:	A dancer of great beauty and grace.
Proteus M. Aurelius:	A scientist and multi-talented artist..

Setting:

Oriented from audience perspective: A large entertainment hall, containing a bar at front-left stage, facing center, with stool seating. A dining table and chairs in middle-center. A couch faces audience at front-right. A small television faces the couch at front-right. A door leads exit middle-right. A wall with paintings follows along far-back to a set of stairs curving up behind the bar at far-left. Front-center stage is open floor.

Part 1:

"A Gathering at Jack's Den"

People surround the stage, chatting, drinking, and laughing. Proteus steps upon a chair and addresses the crowd.

Proteus:

Welcome everyone!

Glad to see such friends in this establishment.
Tis a great joy to congregate for irreverence.

Saltpeter! My man!
Put some drinks in these hands!

It's been a hard day,
and ya'll are worn
in a wicked way.

The demanding world
may cause harm.
But within these walls,
you've no fear at all.

Join in a round,
enjoy the crowd.

Some may get loud,
treat them like your brother.

Relax a bit and feel no pressure.
Many of you could learn of the other.

The day is certainly fleeting drudgery,
yet the night can be high pageantry.
A synthesis of your greatest wishes.

So...
Welcome to another night of bliss.

Not made lightly, this promise,
Or my name is not Proteus!

*[He hops off the chair amidst a smattering of clapping
and laughter. He stops and chats a bit with one of the
participants, and exits by way of the stairs at the back.]*

****

*Seth W. Markowitz nervously taps his fingers at the bar.
He engages the bartender, Saltpeter Faulk.*

Seth:
Hello there sir.
What quality of entertainment
would you have in this establishment?

Saltpeter:
You will find answers to all desires.
And as well the consequences
that follow them, my dear patron.

Seth:

[scanning the room]

A crowd as prismatic as the color calico.

Quite the gathering, though

I tend to keep to myself, generally.

Saltpeter:

Is a party not your regular affair?

Seth:

It is indeed rare.

Though parties do comprise some of my fondest memories...

Yet, there is only so much space in a zero-sum game.

Goodness gracious, indeed!

Memories pondering themselves tend to take up a lot of space.

Thus the task to partition, to discern, conscious intention.

Selective-retro-introspection like historic landmark renovation,

It's psychological urban management.

Hey there's a college course!

[laughing]

I got a Ph.d in that, for sure.

A city of millions, running smoothly.

Should we build a gate or a road,

erect a new building?

Plant crops or a fresh forest?

Ha! Know what I mean?

Like seeds-to-skills,

or practice-in-action,
Even within the mortal dominion,
there are few limits to mental intro-action...
>
> *[nudging Saltpeter]*

If you're into that sort of thing!
>
> *[He laughs.]*

Saltpeter:
>
> *[raising an eyebrow]*

What if I said I was?
>
> *[sizing him up]*

Yes, a strong mind
can fetch a high price.

Perhaps, sir,
you may like to-
>
> *[whispering]*

cash it in?

Seth:
What?

Really?

What would that even entail?
How could anyone...
>
> *[He pauses.]*

What could I get for em?
And which ones anyway?
Does it make a difference?

Saltpeter:

Repayment comes as a blank canvas,

upon which, by this written decree,

I pledge myself to thee,

and my considerable army,

to build the grandest towers,

glorious electric bridges,

plasmic libraries.

That we shall, so to speak,

improve the real estate.

Seth:

Soo... you're going to help me

build cities in my mind?

I thought that was just a metaphor...

Wait a minute-

I still get a hand in what's made.

I get to run the show.

That's a part of the deal.

Saltpeter:

Certainly, good sir!

In fact, as a matter of course...

    [He smiles, produces a letter from his pocket, puts on
spectacles, and begins searching.]

As it would that both parties agree

to whole-heartedly and duly

acknowledge the execution of...

etc., etc.,

da di da da...
In regard to...

Ah! Section 4, part 5, subheading "j": "Grantor shall retain
99.5% of vested interest upon transfer."

Pertaining to this,
I would like to add
that you may partake
in this agreement
an indefinite number
of occasions.

And the action taken
may be either,
or a combination,
of creation and destruction,
limited to a specific memory, or "tract".

(Aside)
        I tell you good ladies and gentlemen,
        tis upon this moment,
        that one begins reeling in the catch...

Seth:
And I get to pick the memory,
or concept, or whatever, right?
        [pondering]

Saltpeter:
As you presently possess

controlling interest, yes.
You may choose which
parcel you wish to cleanse.
And in which space you should like
to rebuild something more impressive,
or practical, or comfortable, or as fantastic
as anything you could imagine.
Or depending on your motivations,
you may wish something more mundane
to take the place of those terrible, unwanted,
invasive, mentally-taxing thoughts.

The choice is yours,
and as far as you will ever know,
the obstructing issue is simply removed.
Your mind will soon operate with renewed vigor,
open to an fresh experiment,
free from chains of past,
and fully liberated.

Seth:
Too often I deal with intrusive thoughts
that slow my creative process.

Yes! The good of the world demands it!

Saltpeter:
We have a winner!
> *[pumping his fist]*

(Aside)
    Ka-ching!
    What did I tell you?

Ahem... excuse me.

You have made a wise choice sir...
    [He produces a tallying machine and a clipboard from behind the bar.]

And upon which parcel
would you like us to begin?

Seth:
Hmm...
let's start by eliminating...
societal conditioning.

Saltpeter:
Ah yes, societ- What? I cannot-
    [He stops writing. The tallying machine clanks and clacks loudly, and it spits out a long ream of paper. *Ding* It stops.]

Sir, that is, ahem...
a tall order.
    [He pauses to read the ticker tape.]
"Societal conditioning," by your meaning,
would take us to dispel,
parcels of grand magnitude.
with reams of contracts,

teams of subjects,

for a great many dedicated periods.

for each hand may only provide,

or acquire so much with each task.

My assistants would work nightly

for a great many of your years

to accomplish this task. Sir.

Perhaps I may suggest

something simpler for the moment?

Seth:

Okay, how's about...

self-doubt.

Saltpeter:

What? That's even worse!

> *[The tallying machine goes berserk. Saltpeter punches
> buttons madly. It finally stops, letting up a small wisp of smoke.]*

Ahem...

Might I suggest the poor memory of,

let us imagine, a scorned love?

That final fleeting moment long lost,

and longer pondered,

perhaps brought by betrayal?

Perhaps your own betrayal...

Seth:

Okay that's enough!
I'm giving you a lot of power here buddy,
don't be snooping through everything.

(Aside)

Jeez, this guy doesn't skip a beat.
[thumbing toward Saltpeter]

I get your point though.
And by the way, my loves
are good memories.
Don't touch those.

Saltpeter:
Fine, fine, sir.
You have my word.
Now please choose
a single, specific memory,
before I change my mind...

Seth:
Okay, a single, specific memory...
Last month I quit my job,
and an executive at "Dingbat Network"
felt the need to pass on some parting words.

Saltpeter:
So you are in show business...

Seth:

Indeed I am, a satirist of current events.

I would prefer to spare you the gory details.

Suffice to say, the memory is a pain.

Get rid of that.

> *[The tallying machine clacks a few times and spits out a short receipt with a satisfying *Ding*.]*

Saltpeter:

An event surely contentious,

best left to the past.

It would be my great pleasure

to relieve you of it.

> *[He nods.]*

Seth:

Good, yes!

Where do I sign?

Surely in blood, right?

Saltpeter:

> *[He laughs.]*

Nothing so dramatic.

When of sound body and mind,

all you require is a simple... drink.

> *[Saltpeter slides a frothy beer toward Seth.]*

Seth:

> *[He pauses, staring at the beverage.]*

Okay, let's do this.

> *[He takes a sip.]*

Whoa! I feel better already!

Hey, I should get to work,
watch an good film or two,
put a fresh coat of paint
on a major monument.
Those mental faculties won't build themselves, right?
> *[laughing]*
Is that the remote for the television?
Do you mind?

Saltpeter:
Not at all, be my guest.
> *[He passes it to Seth.]*
Your desires shall be met in their entirety.
If you so choose to meet them.

Ponder that while you wait,
or dare to partake.

Seth:
Good deal.
I might do that.
> *[Seth walks to the couch and flips on the television.]*

****

> *Tonya Seneca steps up to the bar. She engages Saltpeter.*

Tonya:

So what's there to do around here?
I get the sense you're the man to ask.

I'd get a drink but maybe I'll wait;
there's plenty of boys who'd buy in a heartbeat.

Though I hate to wait on fate,
mostly I enjoy the view.
and one always comes through.

Though when I'm really impatient,
     [mock whispering]
I lock eyes with the biggest shoulder-chip.
     [she laughs]

Saltpeter:
Good to know, miss.
I bet Proteus would take you up on that.

Tonya:
Where did he go?
Why would one,
after welcoming done,
Run off and miss
the fancy goings-on?

Saltpeter:
You may very well
ask him yourself.
Though turned in for a moment,

he will return in time.
Patience as a virtue,
has yet to outlast itself.

And perhaps while waiting,
you may indulge in a libation
of an amber complexion,
topped to perfection,
by the finest of gentlemen.
    [smiling]
Have a drink, and ponder other things.

Tonya:
That's fair,
you old beggar.

Though, I bet you fill
the glass fuller
when you cover the bitters
in odd-tinged powder.

Saltpeter:
My dear woman! To say such a thing!
Were I not averse, I would douse thy blouse!

Such a life you must have led,
to accuse a poor man of the worst of acts.
Is your converse no more than that?

Tonya:

I do not accept the potential as fact.

Simply take note,

I'm watching your back.

Saltpeter:

That is fair,

though my dear,

the possibility you fear,

truly tempts me not.

I assure you, no tricks have I got,

except when clearly disclosed

and performed on the spot.

> *[Saltpeter passes around other drinks. Tonya watches. When he's done, she engages him again.]*

Tonya:

In lieu of what else to do,

why not show me your rue?

Saltpeter:

> *[he laughs]*

You are going to love this...

Ashes to ashes...

> *[He produces a pouch from his jacket, shakes it, and puts his nose in. He pulls it out, wiggles it slightly, and sets the bag down.]*

Dust to dust...

> *[He lights a match with a flourish.]*

And grain to- ACHOO!

[He sneezes a fireball into the air.]
ahem, ah ...flame.
[He bows graciously.]

Tonya:
[applauding]
What a trick!
You're a regular card!
Tell me your name,
that I may know
the man purveying.

Saltpeter:
It is none other than "Saltpeter," my good woman,
and you can guess from whence that came.

Tonya:
Oh yes!
Your moniker's root's thick!
[She laughs.]
People call me Tonya Seneca.

Saltpeter:
Perhaps you have a trick?
To keep with the theme,
one for one is an even shake.

Tonya:
In such a crowded room, and quick?
A spell to whit,

akin to that magic?
Let me think a bit...

Oh yes, how about this:

When I stop moving,
follow my pointed digit
to the object beyond it.
> *[Tonya closes her eyes, clears a bit of room and starts spinning like a ballerina.]*

Watch out, heads up,
kinda blind here people.
> *[She jumps and finishes a fast spin and lands pointing at a pendulum clock. Ding-dong. Ding-dong. It quietly sounds the hour.]*

Saltpeter:
Ahh, wonderful!
So well 'timed',

Quite the trick,
yet there is no risk...

Tonya:
Compared to you,
that is true.
I am guilty as charged,
with less risk to bodily harm,

The real risk is of embarrassment.

In avoiding this, I am naturally gifted.
        [She pauses.]
And look, see this:

There is even more a difference.

Your trick is
mineral and material,
mine, temporal and ethereal.

Opposite, and yet aligned.

Saltpeter:
        [lighting a pipe]
Quite the observation,
A symbiosis of physics.

However, without my material trickery,
you've no body, no chemistry.

Matter and energy fill the voids. indeed.

They remedy the empty,

Tonya:
I am certainly grateful that
eternity were not expended,
solely in its own dimension.

Which is probably

why we came to be,
for without my influence,
you would stay stationary.

Time is the womb which gives birth to your motion.
This notion from which you get action.

Without temporal flow, you've nowhere to go.
No universe, no trees, and no Saltpeter sneeze.

Saltpeter:
I am happy to agree
on this shared utility.
The fairest forces fit well sensibly.

Tonya:
But to go on longer,
we could ask which is the stronger...
    [she growls]

Saltpeter:
Ah, but we have an answer!
Practical symbiosis be damned,
and absolutes be elevated?
    [annoyed]
I would entertain such thoughts.
Though were I a younger man,
and speed were greatest ally,
I would not abide.
The questions of sole thought utility,

so gray, would better wait for a day
when all were free to contemplate.

Tonya:
Very noble of you,
though that statement
appears to conflict with
reality.
For who here is not free to contemplate?
And is this not the place to idly pass time away?
And are you not here to assist in that capacity?

What good a bartender, so unlike the shepherd?
Tending not to his flock, good ones we be,
who ask only lightly to be pleased?

Saltpeter:
Well, to answer frankly,
yes, I am asked to assist.

Yet assistance I will freely,
for my own purposes.

As for tending, you seek my honest thought?
The shepherd need not entertain the flock,
but, rather, sees
to *their* continued reveries.
The space they cross may be his domain,
but from the show, he must abstain.
Talk may indeed enlighten,

but rhetoric does not serve gin.

Tonya:
Ah yes, too busy you be,

Who must I see?

Saltpeter:
Oh, who here
would lend an ear?
        [looking around the crowd]
Try the chap on the couch,
feasting on eye-candy.
There's a ready man willing idly.
        [He points at Seth. Tonya glances.]

Tonya:
Hmm. Maybe.
        [She stands.]
But one more thing:
if you care not entertain,
what do you call that trick with the flame?

Saltpeter:
I believe you call it "icebreaking."

******

Clarence R. Fringe stands at the bar.

Clarence:

Oh ye water of life,

give me strength to

weather these fools,

within and without,

what day and what night.

       [He finishes a beer with a gulp and drinks a shot of whiskey. He sneaks drinks from a few distracted party-goers. He walks to the table and picks up three apples and starts juggling. He jumps between a couple of people having a conversation and promptly spills their drinks with the fruit.]

Bystander:

Hey, what the hell man!

Clarence:

What?

I'm juggling.

Can't appreciate that, plebeian?

Why don't you get out anyway?

No one needs your nay-saying.

Bystander:

You know what?

I like this place,

and I'm not leaving.

What are you going to do, prick?

Clarence:

(Aside)

Such a sort always comes in,
to deny my peaceful whim.
to get the best of thee,
and subvert this vanity.
[to the guy]

Perhaps an obtrusive gringo should
stick his dick in the mashed potatoes?
    [He feigns the act upon a bowl, moaning loudly.]
Ugh, ugh, oh baby, yes!
Oh god! It's so good! Baby!
Yeah, you know it,
you like that prick!
    [in falsetto voice]
Yes, I love it, give it to me!
Give me that love sauce!

Several Party-goers:
What the fuck?
Nasty!

Clarence:
Oh YEAHHHH....
Ahk, ah, ah- YES!
    [He squeezes a bottle of mustard onto the food.]

Partier:
Dude, not cool-

Clarence:

That's right!
[setting the bowl down with a clatter.]
Right on the serving plate-
and in your face!
[He flings a handful at the guy.]
Haha!
How do you like them apples?

Tonya:
[Tonya, fed up with the antics, storms over.]
You enervator! You hater!
Giving seed to starchy puree!
No decency!

Clarence:
Ahh, you have something to say?
[sarcastically]
I live for the flavor, derogatory words, my favorite dish.
Have I done to offend? My open ears, please expand!
They await with anticipation your sweet and sour exhortations.

Tonya:
Say more than once?
I pronounce you a dunce.

By this slight to all.
I declare you foul, weak,
and unworthy of feast!

Clarence:

Ah! Just what I needed.
There's a jolt of serotonin!

Oh wonderful woman,
pray tell of my horrid persuasions.
Beneath you, I bow,
that your righteous whip allow.
     [He bows to her on his knees.]
My skin, to you, doth now belong.
Treat it harsh, become it strong.

Tonya:
I care not your submission...
Taste this boot and split!
     [She kicks him.]

Clarence:
Yes, more, my mistress!
Do not deny me the truth of it!

Ow! Hey, that's starting to hurt!

Tonya:
Your sorry hide, I will whip!
Take off, or you'll get the worst of it!
     [Clarence backs away.]
Now remove yourself from my sight!
and know you got off light.
Listen...
     [putting her hand to her ear]

Not a hint of laughter,

You're a failure of a prankster!

> *[Clarence exits the door. Smattering of yelaughter.]*

Party-Goer:

> *[going up to hug Tonya and thank her]*

Nicely done!

Tonya:

> *[stepping back]*

Oh, sorry, you kind of got something you...

Party-goer:

> *[laughing]*

Oh yeah, right. Thanks.

Potatoes and fucking mustard, man...

> *[He walks away, wiping with his shirt.]*

Tonya:

(Aside)

> There's a nutty joker who will deliver,
> however, come with fewer presents,
> and more cock than acquiescence.
>
> Feels like you gotta stay vigilant.
> with justice and employ.
> to keep in place the lower droogs,
> men and boys,
> who frequent these gatherings,

Hmm, that guy over there.

The same Saltpeter did name,

watching the pictures moving.

His eye is surely keen,

to follow the lines he sees,

the stories that please.

He may come recommended well,

but I shall tell

a smile,

from a spell.

[She walks to the couch. Seth W. Markowitz intently watches the television. Tonya sits beside him. She fiddles with something on the coffee table. She makes motions in the air with her fingers. She stands up, performing splendors, spins, slithers, bends, Seth is unfazed. She decides to block his view.]

Tonya:

Hey big boy, what's your story?

[Seth leans to his left.]

Fancy attraction in another direction?

[She blocks his view.]

My thoughts and attention belay

dancing-in-waiting your way...

[Seth leans to his right.]

Heard from your friend,

an ear you would lend...

[She blocks his view.]

The name's Tonya,

and fine you forget it.

If needed, other times

chance remembrance.

> *[Seth leans back left.]*

But in this second...

> *[Back and forth they go.]*

on this day...

> *[Faster.]*

by way you...

> *[...]*

I pursue...

> *[...]*

if for a moment...

> *[...]*

you may...

> *[Tonya gets fed up.]*

look away!

> *[She opens her blouse to cause his attention.]*

Seth:

Yes?

Oh, wow.

> *[He finally sees her.]*

You must be cold in that dress.

> *[She laughs.]*

A blanket here, I offer.

I hope it may proffer friendship

or a higher form of it.

I may be focused, but only so

creative buds do grow.

From the masters we may learn,

their cause, our future turn.

Yet I say nuts
to the classically-taught,
anxiety-ridden,
explicit derision,
wicked fixation...!

So you say,
established technique.
For true gems of artistic beauty
are meant to be seen.
And you know, at best,
artists' works go far beyond jest.

Tonya:
Hey, there you are!
Thought for a moment you lost radar.

I see why you're invested deeply,
But come now a moment,
forget the television.
Have you tried an investigation
of the *personal* dimension?

Seth:
My life does not revolve around the screen;
indeed, it revolves around me.
Yet the search for truth sails many seas.
Don't you think it worth comprehending,

the great works of humanity?
Given so many of us,
and so fewer distillers,
worth it not, to take stock?

Tonya:
I do not deny the utility,
but the perspective pales in comparison.
See?
>*[She displays herself.]*
I am more worthy than she.

My boy, I stand before thee,
and speak more than mere pleasantries.
Take what you would of works,
but life is the real artistry.

Watch what you like,
and like what you do,
but this life, is here,
right in front of you.

Shall I perform an ancient story, perhaps?
One full of guts and glory and heroic tasks?

Seth:
How delightful.
Absolutely!

Tonya:

I shall begin,
some millennia past,
when monsters and men
both lived abreast.

*[Tonya tells the story with appropriate gestures,
projecting shooting spears, giant marauding monsters, fights,
fires, and other things.]*

Mastodons roamed
in forest and savanna both,
while human you know
hid within sheltering home.

When night did come,
enormous beasts sought sustenance,
and no one, even today,
could count the death of so many,
brought upon our ancestors
by fanged and clawed marauders.

One inventive sort, born keen, smart and sharp,
did turn his work to weapons, arming his brethren.
One attack after another, they rebuffed,
such the toothy predators
challenged no longer,
their spirit the stronger.

Now rest at night, his people could,
and protect their gathering bands in the wood.

Soon ability grew, and upon their backs armor,

carved from the skin and bone of beasts slaughtered.

Established dominance, and ready for all malice,
gathering turned to hunting, a glorious challenge.

The beasts, in these stories, drove a brave many
toward greater glories, to find the abodes from whence
they descend, and take the fight to their own den.

Many dragon-slayers were born in such eons,
driven by glory and righting past wrongs.

But soon the ice came, and with it cold,
driving the conquering warlords home.

Another young sort tried his hand,
mind alight and crackling,
sought the secret to the spark set by lightning.

The cold was a greater beast,
but could not defeat with spear nor sling.

Ingenuity tamed the ephemeral enemy,
and lit the night with fire's light.

In control now,
but little gathering to be found,
new creatures clamored about.

With ice so thick,

hunting was the trick.

The fires were lit and the flint did glint!

You could not imagine the hunting parties those days:
Hungry and determined,
our ancient kin painted
the snow red with conquest.

But they did not know,
that with great feasting,
trouble is in tow.

They relied on meat for their bread.
but comprehended less, its regeneration.

So many victories at their hands,
but ever worse were the starving masses.

They tried in vain, with more slayers sent,
but not with meat, if at all, they came back.

A famine befell, and many perished.

And now, fewer beasts, this world, inhabit.

Indeed content, we must be,
with the deer, the squirrel, and the rabbit.
  [Laughter and some clapping from a few onlookers.]

Seth:
Brava!
Grand story of the past!

Truth be told,
I've seen them all,
and with each story
the more remote the glory.

Tonya:
So, you like it?
  [Seth nods.]
But what are you trying to say...?

Seth:
  [He leans back.]
Here you decide a moment derived.
Wherever located, it is arbitrarily denoted.
  [Laugh track sounds from the television and begins to respond to Seth's words.]

Lifetimes and lifelines twist alongside,
interconnected, yet distant from the present.

It simply lacks connection to contemporary.

Your audience barely lives
within the reach of their noses.

For adulation,
the critic would say:

"appeal to their sensibilities,
or all effort is mistaken."
> *[He snickers and takes a drink.]*

How's that make your story worthy?
> *[Ooo's and gasps from the television.]*

Tonya:
Watch, sir, please, your tempora-centrism.
How in the world can you know the best,
without the mindset of your ancestral band,
who struggled for the good life,
against such strife?

And further, call yourself a critic,
who critiques not the words and deeds acted,
but the utilization of marketing tactics.

How far you must have fallen,
deep into a pool of modern stupor,
using business language as sole rebuke.

If rendered speechless ye be,
carry that sentiment as a sign of merit,
and do not judge for lacking tact
in the market of artifice.

If little critique I draw,
do not strain to perform that duty.
It is far too obvious to those watching.
> *[television "ooo"s]*

Seth:

[clearly surprised]

Well, okay, fine,

if you must squeeze a ripened mind-

Tonya:

Over-ripe, if to spill so sour-

Seth:

Say what you will,

but do it elsewhere.

You've won the match, love.

And in defeat,

I return to my research.

Tonya:

(Aside)

Games and sets we play,

dominating for solitary reward.

I care not for a lonely throne,

victors garner victims.

Exemplary feats, I perform,

yet ever more, must procure.

Are you not a man?

[Gasps from audience.]

A man you must be.

Within, I see a flame.
Light tinder and roar,
for sake of justice!

Hold not your tongue!
Or excuse me
if such a whelp you be.

Seth:
(Aside)
How dare she!

Damn me,
for what?

Priceless structures
beyond any others,
utilizing the full capacity
of a mastermind.

Then again...
How could anyone else know the extents,
the planning and the effort expended,
exacted upon a mind,
to create the human we see,
without documenting it?

Damn me?! For infinity?
She knows not the lengths,
the knowledge gained and contained,

in this precisely constructed-

Damn me!

It's not enough to give mere description.
Her point passes the challenge on, however,
to evoke an expenditure of combined labor,
and exercise the boon of the mind's endeavors.

A mere intaker?
I shall speak my war and peace.
[Seth stands and speaks forcefully.]

I've seen the heights of artistic pride,
and know what is good and right,
I create with reasonable stakes.

I've joined the grand roll,
I'm a part of it all!
>*[Audience cheers.]*

Tonya:
(Aside)
>No man an island.

But when merely spoken, without action,
grand words lean to wickedness.
Still little sense. Prove it hence.

Seth:

You demand of evidence?
If you have not seen it yet,
I proclaim you ignorant!

My name is Seth W. Markowitz,
upon critical comedy you see it attached.

I make biting wit, taking vengeance,
tearing down oppressive proclamations!

The highest of the high now hold their tongues,
for Seth is here with loaded gun,
ammo pulled from lying boasts,
cleaned of spittle and re-purposed,
to fire back, at the priest,
the politician, and the quack.

They know the stone's throw can crack.
And each piece I make,
the greater brick I create!
     [Audience cheers.]

Tonya:
(Aside)

     Good work he may do, it's true.
     With this, I have no issue.

     Yet for curiosity's sake,
     I will implore him further,
     and find where lies

his ultimate gate.

Observe...
[to Seth]

I am sure that it is all great.
crafting a better purpose from projectiles awry-aimed.
But what when few deplorables your foe doth make?

Could you,
of the pure clay,
make something true?
[Audience "Oooo"s.]

Seth:
Fie woman! It could not be so!
You speak of a perfect world as if it were tomorrow!

I am quite content to meter justice, if momentarily.

Were the case, as you say, the day came
without those human mockeries,
and fine we be for all eternity?

Let that day come at me.
I stand ready to improve the surroundings.

Have I satisfied your inquiries?
My attention strays to researching.
[Seth sits back down.]

Tonya:

One more word, quickly!

Rarely with notables, I converse.

One point still sticks; and if wrong, correct me.

The clown plays against the straight man, no doubt;

yet what does the clown do when the straight man is out?

Seth:

What does the clown do when...

> *[He trails off, pauses for a moment. The television laughs and jeers derisively at him.]*

(Aside)

> A motley hue colors my pride?
> Detestable figures be motivators,
> yes, and what of I?
> The cart behind their horse?

> Secondary energy to
> stooges and rubes
> masquerading as true,
> and Seth, the best,
> a mere sideshow?
> No.

> This fortune is *not* complete.
> You shall leave this seat, see the past
> as practice, and set the present to victory.
> *[Seth walks to the television and it starts to quiet down. He puts his face near the screen and touches the flickering*

*characters. He runs his hands around the box, feeling the shape
and form of it, with a newfound understanding. Television
audience chuckles nervously.]*

(Aside)

Researching...
Reruns and replays,
never-ending cavalcades,
carnival parades of judgment,
dramatic reenactments,
perpetuating past rivalries,
regurgitating stagnant stories,
directing manipulation,
and placing blame on participation.

You made this happen!
You demanded the fool entertain!

For without actualization,
art is mere distraction.

Night after night, day after day,
the king becomes the fool's plaything.
The master unwittingly willed to serve.

And if a fool you be,
you've insisted fully on your folly,
perhaps enough to become wise...

Tonya:
What are you doing?

[She steps away, tip-toeing backward.]

Seth:

[The television audience starts to panic, as if running from a burning building.]

My studies-
[He picks the television up, the heavy thing...]
are complete!
[...and smashes it to the floor.]
You placater, you denier!

You hypnotizing, horrid polluter!
[He hefts a wooden chair.]
You brain-washing, hegemonizing monster!
[He brings it down on the busted television.]
You insidious, hazardous, vacuous projector!
[Smashing, smashing]
You zip-twisted, machine-headed brick!
[Smashing, chair breaks, smashing]
Take that!

You tyrant!
[The party quiets. Seth stops. He looks about, wild-eyed. All eyes are upon him. He looks down at the wreck. Looks back up.]

Seth:
That was a long time coming.
[He coughs, straightens his shirt, and bows graciously.]
Thanks for watching.

[Smattering of laughter. Seth sits. After a moment, he takes a notepad, and begins writing.]

****

Part II:

"Synergy in the Key of Swing"

Bystander:
That was awesome!

Bystander:
Yeah, that shit was asking for it!
Rage the cage!

Bystander:
Rage the cage!

Alexander D. Cellini steps out of the crowd.

Alexander:
You want rage?
I got your rage right here!

Rage the cage and send the
trash to the compactor!

Had enough celluloid dreams, have you?
Those spectral heads telling what to who?
Rage the cage indeed!

Grab the bars and shake, file that bitch away!
Smash what with what hammer!
Take up implements, the ones you know best!
Beat the wall, scrape the bars, vibrate and shake
to the foundations, the base!
Break these walls of fool's gold!
     [The crowd cheers.]
Had enough of it yet? Have you?
I got your rage pulsing through my carotid artery.
Coursing and rushing, veins inter-taking,
dumping waste and picking up steam!

This house is cardboard furniture,
and soaking, all the better!
To slice through,
a simple blade will do.
     [He takes a decorative sword off the wall.]
By this or by that,
take up your implements!
     *[Party-goers take up weapons of sorts: a pocket knife, a
dinner plate, a frying pan, a wooden chair, etc.]*
This cage shall be rattled
and dashed to bits!
God help me!
     [He stabs the sword into the wall, and lets it sit.]
Now who here's got the guts?
Not to fight inanimate objects,
but tear at the very
heart of malevolence?

There is a plot about us all.

Controlled by draconian freaks?
No, just another metaphor.

The assassination of our leaders,
now there's a pattern.
Don't need shadowy possibility
when you got *history*.

Guess who's holding you back?
Bohemian Grove idolaters? No.
Illuminati? Just indicators.

Labels and stables of horse
and rider reared to practice avarice,
nepotism in ignorance.

And worse still,
they don't even see
that they are bettered
by degree
with you and me.

Freemasonry?
Sounds like a club of buddies,
round a stone table, carved gracefully,
guarding secrets of ancient technology.

The real malignant factors
are systemic detractors
playing hands in the game of sway.

And played for what?
A question of philosophy.
Answer it today!

Those gawkers and squawkers on the television
are easy conversations for suburbanite children,
yet ultimately empty and purposely devoid of meaning.
Good then, to see a proper smashing in this setting.

Don't do them the courtesy
of attentive pleas, even in derision,
for all news is good news
in Westboro Baptist Church pews.

I see a grand new fashioning,
not aspiring to entertaining,
but affecting and *effecting*.
Too many youth's dreams are pretending!
And where began that sentiment?

Funded and propped by the very unsplendid,
wicked tricksters, hoodwinking to serving.
Had enough yet, have you?!

Bystanders:
Yeah!

Alexander:
Well now,
Who's got the guts for it?

It's a dirty business making amends.
Sometimes you cut at the seams.

The Bilderberg Group? You already know who goes.
The names ain't secret, but guess what? You ain't in it.

The highest on the ladder, a country club gathered round
shared motivation, securing position,
status quo self-preservation.

They don't give a shit about you,
enshrined by faux-virtue!

Intelligent men in the past
found rationale in their avarice,
with basal desires as foundation,
built speculations into a house,
stacked against those out-of-bounds,
not the least of whom, and more the most,
argue the necessity of forced control
in an endless hierarchy.

Where does that leave you and me?

Scuttling about, little constructors,
repairing holes in the masonry.
Termites at the bidding of the queen,
fashioning shackles for slavery!

The true house chewed and digested,

to make conical nests infested.

Wise up, and you could be selected,
to queen a colonial destination,
and get unjust desserts
off the back of foreigner's work,
while extracting free
from the true house of plenty.

My friends, don't you see?
Repeating is not a fault, when repeating we need.
Though apparently, the concept has yet to be absorbed fully.

You don't need conspiracy when you have history!

Forty years, at least, carving away freedom of speech,
justice, education, equal opportunity, and privacy;
slavery transposed-economically,
persecuting minorities,
and perpetuating tragedies.

Disaster capitalism at its apex!

In absence of the good fight,
fights nonetheless,
and takes Vietnam, Afghanistan,
and Iraq.

Legitimacy disregarded for
a shiny car and a gilded prison.

Knowledge with a penalty,
raising the cost for every scholar
and every ship.

Don't think you can escape it,
they've hamstrung our generation.

Maggie's Farm is open for business.

Don't like it?
There's the door and the street floor,
where you'll scrounge for a living,
kicked and beaten,
reviled and on trial for being poor.

Until finally ruled a cautionary tale,
by some contemporary Hans Christian.

Some fairy tale, some yarn that's spinning,
to scare the wits out the menially living.
The worse at the bottom, the more the pushing
to scare for fear of calamity,
the most-manipulable feeling,
sets us salivating,
like Pavlov's bell-ringing.

Scared by naught and ignorant of ought,
the "powers that be" cling to yesterday,
employing exceptional madness,
to preserve traditional tactics,

squeezing an iron fist tighter,
round a palm-full of water.

Now who's got the guts?!

To pull the guts out,
and set them back intact?

Who's the team of cut,
     [retrieving the sword]
and who's the team of sew?
     [raising it up]
No matter what,
we could use you.

    [He slices into the wall. He hacks at it again, making a hole, and another. The others join in, beating on the wall. Plastic slinkies fall out. PVC pipe. Alarm clocks. Blenders. Phones. Miniature cars. Army men. Toy guns. Real guns. The wall is thick with items. They come spilling out into a great pile. People rush around and about, picking things up and examining, puzzling over the bonanza.

    Alexander is the last one to stop, scraping the sword and scratching, prying at the cracks in the brick outer wall. He sees a sledgehammer and picks it up. He is about to swing when someone stops him.]

Party-goer:
Hey, whoa man, ease up,
I don't know you want to bust that up.
Those bricks keep the cold out, the ceiling up.

And besides, look what we've done!

Alexander:

[He pauses, looks over the great spillage of things, nods at her, drops the hammer with a clang, and readdresses the crowd.]

See what come of the freedom
'tween and beyond every wall?
[sifting through the items]
Look, a branch, a grain-stalk.
The stone. The clock.
The fuel. Chemical charge.
Look at all this!
What are we going to do with them?
How do we arrange it all?

Every one a tool or spoil,
great and minor;

We must temper them!

And this...

Look! A new manifestation.
[Alexander places a glowing green orb on the table so it does not roll about, and begins examining the object.]

****

The party has mixed reactions of joy and bewilderment. Some have taken to playing with the new-found devices, symbols, Saltpeter had been watching quietly from behind the bar.

Saltpeter:

(Aside)

>Quite the development, I might say.
>Looks like they've found their toys.
>I thought I had hid them better than that.
>*[speaking above the crowd]*

It's alright everyone! Calm yourselves.
Didn't you know these things were around?

They are all yours, of course.
A feast of trinkets and spoils
of some thousand years.

Yes, yes, the whole of history,
the most wondrous devices imaginable,
all great things, of course.
>*[he pauses]*
Don't bother about it much,
there's a party to be done.

Wait for tomorrow's sober moments
to fiddle with these implements.

To follow the metaphor, 'sew'?
Please, in your state? Ha!

For the morning, it can wait.
>*[He kicks away a guy's hand reaching for a grenade.*
>*He grabs his shirt and dresses him down. Then puffs his pipe*
>*gruffly.]*

Call me the devil but not suicidal!

[Clarence sneaks back in from the front door. He is wearing sunglasses, a fake beard, and a different shirt.]

Clarence:

Oh my, dear me!

What a splendid spree!

Hey you, I'll take that, see.

[grabbing a toy from a kid]

I get the goods here.

Haha!

[the kid pouts]

Aww, you really wanted it?

I'll snap it in half!

[He breaks the toy and dusts off his hands.]

(Aside)

A vast improvement

on that sorry figure,

I just did him a favor.

[He walks to the bar.]

Haha! Bartender, my man!

A pint of your finest ale, snap snap!

Saltpeter:

Yes, "your foolishness."

[pouring Clarence the drink]

You seem to have gotten your just desserts,

and I shall trust you've learned the error of your ways.

You're free to trade, but
this is your last warning to
keep your dick out the buffet,

Clarence:
No worries my man!
[He takes a deep drink and nearly finishes the glass.]
There's always your mom's vadge.

Saltpeter:
[enraged]
WHAT?!

Clarence:
[unassumingly]
Though it could'a been better.
Next time, I'll use more butter.

Saltpeter:
Now, you are not getting another.
Fact of the matter, better
take your butter-loving hide
out of this establishment
or I'll scatter your ashes
over my garden plants!
*[Saltpeter gulps a shot of strong liquor, flicks a lighter
and a spits a fireball at him. Clarence freaks out, backs away and
disappears into the crowd.]*

No one speaks of my mother like that!
[Tonya gets a drink at the bar.]

Tonya:

He is such a creep.

Jeez, you're fuming!

Saltpeter:

Were I as low a form as he,
I would scorch his entrails...

Tonya:

Oookay...

> *[She goes to Alexander, entranced by the orb, and pulls up a chair beside him.]*

Tonya:

Hey you!
Mister Revolution!
What a speech!
That was amazing.
Did you know there was
all of this?!
In there?

> *[Alexander does not respond.]*

Hey, what's with the bubble sphere?

Looks like green jelly in there.
Can it float, high in the air?
Does it spark from anywhere,
lightning at your touch?
Throw thunderbolts like old gods?
Does it carry the flame,

of kerosene or butane,
billow warmth from winter hearths?

Can you bowl it,
as a ball, to strike pins?
Does it spin about
when you press its buttons?
Can it lead a path through the wilderness,
as a lamp, atop a scepter-staff?

Can it talk back?
Answer your query matter-of-fact?
> *[to the ball]*
I have a question for you ball,
can you answer a simple yes or no?
> *[The ball is silent.]*
Fine, be like that.
> *[to Alexander]*
How bout you friend?
Your thoughts on the sphere?
Has it spoken to thee?
> *[Alexander is silent.]*

(Aside)
> And it happens again.
> What is it with men,
> all focused on projects?

Hey, you! Wake up!
> *[She grabs him by the shirt and shakes roughly.]*

Alexander:

Ahh, eh gads!

[He looks away, hesitantly, and then blinks, toward her, unfocused.]

Excuse me a moment,
while I adjust to the surroundings.
This, that thing, is quite involving.

What's that you were saying?

Tonya:

What's with the orb,
something within?

Alexander:

Within it, that is...
When you look at it...
It's ahh...
I don't quite understand it,
some kind of magic.

Like a rushing river
of scenic layers,
it predicts and assists,
a dream-weaving kaleidoscope
of gameplay and invention.

It works with your thoughts
and shapes to your wish.

Did you try it?
Look.

Tonya:
[puzzled]
It reads the thoughts you give,
when entranced in it?
That's different.
Any physical manifestations?
Can it connect electronic?

Alexander:
I don't know, haven't tried.
Give a look from that side.
[Tonya stares intently into the orb.]
Stare at a single point,
and the inside gets cloudy,
with muddy curves and swirls,
frilly motions and smokey tendrils,
then, like liquid mercury
solidifies into figures of your making.

Try to ignore the peripheral blur.
Is it happening?

Just a bit longer...

****

(If no video or representation possible, use narrator here.)

With a strange rapidity, the gluid solidifies, into bricks and curvy structures. Little men and women, trees and streets snake about through the air, toward a larger constructed door, spinning and swirling toward the area of her focus, seeing a young girl playing, a kite, a swing. And the ground opening, fire within. She dances toward it, a tectonic shift to magma, skipping and laughing, she edges closer but does not notice. [Tonya gasps.] A string, a rope appears in her outstretched hands, and she drifts over the volcanic rift, and lands on a magic carpet. She floats above her home, above the city proper, hovering above it. Suddenly, the carpet rips. [She gasps again] An eagle catches her. It soars higher, higher, enough to see the whole earth. Planets, the solar system spreads out before. Full expanse. [She twists about.] It becomes a wavy pattern, then a black slate, spinning in various dimensions, two, then three, in different perspectives, shifting and morphing to her intentions, consciously creating a shifting, constructing soup of tiny beads, forming into a human figure with long, wavy hair, standing.

[She shifts.]

A 3D printer that someone was fiddling with suddenly springs to life. Tonya wrenches herself away from the orb. She notices Alexander's hand on her leg.

Tonya:

Quite presumptuous of you.

But I do not disagree.

So long as you contain yourself

to where the sun doth see.

Alexander:

I thought some

relaxation of the body,

might confer as much

to the mind.

118

Tonya:

You do presume,
of course.

Yet right as ever,
to presume right,
is quite clever.
> *[She purrs.]*

Alexander:

You never know until you do.
And I'm happy to come through
with an accurately estimated pursuit.
> *[He smiles.]*

So what do you think:
is the sphere grand or middling?
Distracting or invigorating?
The pictures and shapes, changing states,
do they spur ingenuity and sate curiosity?

Tonya:

It is quite astonishing,
and I did try something different,
perhaps there is evidence.

I tried to make material.
and another machine,
was responsive to my signal.

Alexander:

I'll check it out.

[Alexander wanders around the devices littering the back half of the room. He chats a bit with some of the people examining them. He goes to a 3D printer running on another table and speaks to an onlooker admiring the machine, watching it build something.]

The lady, over yonder, spake her mind
within and without the orb of power.
Did it start just now, or some time other?

Onlooker:
All of a sudden, a second ago,
before you showed.
There's no electricity,
that is, far as I can see.
Was giving the once over,
twice at that moment,
when out of thin air,
came a sensation,
quite potent.
Tweaked my nerves a bit,
to be honest.

But wait til the boys
get a load of this:
shiny, smooth, clean,
and not one bit of electricity.
[grasping the machine possessively]

What you say about an orb of power?

Alexander:

Thank you,

I wouldn't worry about it.

> *[he returns to Tonya]*

Good god, lady!

See what you've done!

The machine over here began printing something,

and it doesn't even have electricity.

Tonya:

> *[Tonya goes to the printer, watching it gyrate, creating a figurine.]*

Ah ha! It works!

Beyond divination,

complete actualization!

Wonder machines!

Alexander:

You got that right.

Tonya:

Quite the development, this is.

Devices that interact with the thoughts,

communicate decisively, intentionally,

transferring signal and electricity.

This is not illusory.

Alexander:

Is it what you meant it to be?

Tonya:
It's a decent facsimile.

Alexander:
How did you apply it thus?
What did you use
to transfer and infuse?

Tonya:
I suppose it's simple enough
to make hardware of thoughts.

The orb gives first observational power:
thermal receptors of the viper,
magnetic sense of the swallow.
and the dolphin's sonic echo.

Each electrical machine in range
shined an interpretable wave,
I saw the printer earlier,
and thought in that direction
without obstruction.

The energy was inherent,
and crossed space inerrant.
Some internal source
supplied the force.

Then, like a game of hearts,
the particles played

and plied their trade
at super-speed,
crossing bridges
and pathways,
if/thens, U-turns,
tracks and pens.

Then like water along the shoals.
the signal flowed back and forth.

Alexander:
Quite the development, very much so.
The proof is here for this truth.
We should explore further.

In that respect, however,
the orb speaks to thee
much more than me.

Tonya:
     [wrapped up in the implications]
What does this mean?
By thought alone, we may effect something!

Tools are breaking inherent divides
of fundamental metaphysics,
philosophy of mind, evident duality,
separation of consciousness from reality...

Maybe that's why some abhor technology.

and argue for, the so-called,"better part of valor"

And yet here we are,
inevitably drawn
from yesterday to now.

Every minute progress researches a finer edge,
slicing object and subject, irrespective.

Implication becomes demonstration,
less work for more action,
These labor's fruits
carry heavy ethics.

No beneficence from simple existence,
but through intent and execution.

Our fascination with invention,
paves the road to hell and heaven.
As the pendulum crosses our path,
we can reflect on each swing's effect,
and perhaps avoid the worst of the swing-backs.
[She pauses in thought.]

Alexander:
This is beyond practical invention,
applied toward labor's reduction.

Akin to the progression of knowledge,
tech stands upon the shoulders of giants,

for, without the greatest flame
one cannot harness the lightning.

Atlas and Prometheus,
held immobile and rigid,
gave us lofty vantage,
and allowed a height
that we may test flight,

No longer attached to Earthly pillars,
and with each new tool, we supersede the other.

If only similar progress
were pursued in politics...
     [He pauses.]
Where be the judge of the peace?
War has him in a stranglehold.
Even dropped to a knee,
he cannot breathe,
but only wait,
for hate to hyperventilate.

Even a thousand cuts cannot
bring about its surrender.
     *[Alexander watches a couple people laugh and joke with
a handgun.]*

This patience weathers.
It seems forever to effect the better.
     [He sighs.]

Tonya:

   [She rubs his back, her head on his shoulder.]
Patience...
That word be a sprite and a songstress.
To finish the debate,
yet only to lie in wait.

The tongue's tip tastes sugar sweet,
but only momentarily,
for longer lasts the bitter in the back,
and sour at the sides.

Here, have a sip,
and let life temper
your patience.

Alexander:

   [Alexander drinks from her cup.]
Yes, a momentary respite.

Tonya:

And in the meanwhile, perhaps,
you may like to practice?
To create with the orb?
It is exciting, for sure.

Alexander:

Exciting for some, it may be,
yet short-lived for me,
as little difference 'tween it and my dreams.

I would soon find myself like that other fellow.
    [He indicates Seth.]
Finally thrashing at the self-reflection
with its grand promise a greater deception.

Besides, I live for other things.

Tonya:
I know what you mean.

And even the greatest creation
always leaves one wanting.
    [She sighs.]

Alexander:
    [He turns to face her.]
That's always been enough for me,
crafting something of the clay.

Yet side shows
stage not
the major play.
    [He leans closer to her, touches her neck, and speaks deliberately.]

Trinkets and baubles,
of them, one can be master.
But toys make poor partners.

    [The party fades out to a spotlight on the couple.
They get close and quiet for a few moments and walk upstairs

together. They exit through the door. Clarence follows. He puts his ear to the door.]

Clarence:

(Aside)

Ahh, two birds in the codling tree.

Oh so sweet!

I bet rambunctious sorts in the sheets.

[he laughs]

Where could be...

[He sees a keyhole beneath the doorknob.]

Ah yes! A window to the inside!

What are they doing? I must spy...

[He looks through it, singing and rubbing himself.]

A couple, oh so lovely...

A couple, oh so lovely...

Draws the gaze with certainty,

a true feast for the body!

To watch is my solemn duty.

A couple, oh so lovely.

Warms the cockles with pleasure,

neither purchased nor rendered.

Tis indeed free!

A couple, oh so lovely.

Do they desire your eye?
They must so wish,
for they are not selfish!

A couple, oh so lovely.

I raise a post to thee,
a couple, oh so lovely...
[Clarence starts reaching into his pants.]

****

Part III:
21st Century X New Roman

Bang!

The door slams open. Clarence tumbles down the stairs and limps away, half naked from the waste down, into the crowd.

Madonna della Verità steps out, quite stately, the very definition of beauty. Long legs, golden hair, a queen, dressed in immaculate finery. She descends a curving staircase toward the party. With every step, the ruckus quiets measurably. Heads turn slowly, voices drop to hushed whispers. The party turns to her. She gives signs effortlessly, a touch of her dress, swing of her hair, and signals with her hands, positions of truth and wisdom. A glowing aura surrounds her, as if tinged electric. Her touch is warm. Spirits lift and wounds heal. Her presence is like holy water for the parched. She is fluid motion, gliding as on ice. The music changes tune to her dance. She calls out and addresses the crowd.

Madonna:

Ladies and gentlemen,
pleased to make your acquaintance.

I live in your dreams, no question,
yet I am no exception.
I am your willing model, if you wish.
I stand before you all, a gift.

However,
not a mere trinket,
that sits 'til you spin it.
Not a painting hung above the mantle,
nor sculpture upon pedestal.
Not a mannequin for clothes to fit,
nor doll with angel-hair strands,
embodying hopes or dreams or fantasies,
to be, or to be with, me.

I am no static reflection of heaven.
No Luna of the night,
for I create my own light.

Endowed with blessings
and an inclusive touch,
　　　　[She brushes along the onlookers.]
How about it?
That feel electric?
Do these lips call to thee?
On what part of your body

could you deny me?

Bells ring, angels sing for beauty.
Living as much within you as me.
You pine and strive to find it,
and oh how tongue-tied you get!
      [She grazes another stupefied onlooker with her hand.]
Is this gaze so sultry,
this form so lovely,
this bodacious body,
so full of bubbly...

Does this fizz tickle your fancy?

All because of little old me?
Ha!

It's all fun and games, really.
But beware the rues
jealousy's tricks play.

A double-edge sword, swung either way,
the ego compares the outsider,
and fights to preserve a pecking order.
Constant competition
conflicts with our nature, within.

And it boils my blood to see it used so.
True ideals
callously paraded

for neither virtue, nor celebration,
but commercial abuse and exploitation,
expending blessings on excessive vanities,
and promoting pursuits borne of envy.
Seeking the fountain of youth in perpetuity,
with the fountain of truth right in front of thee.

Beauty knows no age, nor color,
no size, nor luster.
no upbringing, nor schooling,
no occupation, nor geographic location.

You may envy my particular shape,
but my abode is only that,
where one lives, a matter of fact.

What you see is simply
the most visible
aspect I inhabit.

And you've heard it before,
'beauty in the eye of the beholder'.
yet there is so much more.
For what when the eye looks upon the mirror?
Is that beauty clear?
Or is it fleeting as leaves in the wind,
blinking out as mirage in near distance?
Does the eye grow tired with each advance,
until finally collapsing to the sand?

Only in the desert of the empty eye.
For beauty's bottom stretches deep,
and gives birth to infinite variety.

Beauty lives within all of thee!

Nurture well its seed,
whether in eye or chest,
in light or in breath,
in spirit or in mind.

Fulfill the feeling,
that it may
weather the desert.
Celebrate with fervor!

Merely the eye of the beholder?
It is the tree, the water, and the gardener.

> *[She finishes with a bow, and the crowd whoops and hollers.]*

Onlookers:
Huzzah!

I got her next drink!

Cheers to the Lady!

> *[She walks to the bar.]*

Saltpeter:
Madonna Della Verita,

we had hoped you would come.

[slightly bowing]

Might I offer thee a glass
our finest champagne?

[displaying the bottle]

Madonna:

I should love as much, certainly.

[Saltpeter pops it.]

Saltpeter:

For you, my dear.

[setting the glass in front of her]

Tis a treat, quite rare, to hear,
eloquent words from one so fair.
You seem to have, in all honesty,
moved through and beyond false modesty.
As such, your wisdom rivals your beauty.

Madonna:

Why thank you!
Your compliment is well met.

And now that you mention it,
endowments seem rarely exclusive,
but come with a motley crew assorted.
The trick is to keep the eyes open,
drop blinders of too narrow focus,
and behold the beauty beyond the surface.

Brings to mind the notion
of the "well-rounded" person.

> *[She traces the outline of her body in the air.]*

Saltpeter:
To reveal the myriad of surfaces,
one chips away the rough edges.

> *[He polishes a cylindrical glass to a shine, holding it to the light.]*

The cube will sit static,
while the stone rolls dynamic.
Though to use it requires turning vigilant.

Madonna:
Ah but is it an even worse fate to watch,
poor Sisyphus roll a box?

Saltpeter:
That unlucky fellow is all caught up
in making the job hard on himself.
He is tallying and counting every step
of a never-ending task!
No condition of his sentence
included anything like that.

Madonna:
I wonder, what does it take
to impart truth of autonomous fate?

Words and speech can relate,

but do great deeds inspire the same?

Or are we merely happy
witnessing a break in monotony?

Saltpeter:
You ask lone Saltpeter?
That truth can be devastating,
and the "fate you make"
may fall flat on its face.

I will tell you,
when I tend
to troubles and woes,
some are the product of inaction,
but more so ignorance of the present.
For when once upon a moment,
someone missed a point,
and my poor patron pines and aches
to take another choice.

Here they ponder, weak and weary,
and regret washes over like a tsunami.
Jim and John and Wendy,
caught in a pool whirling steadily,
and chasing ghosts,
that even in pictures,
look fuzzy.

Meanwhile, pondering the very regrets

that keep them coming.
Caught in the moment on repeat,
like a fresh record on a broken player.

Like prolific musicians,
some patrons create great libraries,
yet hardly get a listen,
for the broken machine is the only one working.

Speaking of which, I should probably get that fixed...

Madonna:
What a cacophony!
Perhaps the answer is forward thinking?

Saltpeter:
For many,
true happiness is as rare
as a bird of paradise in winter.

Their quest is of an ultimate nature,
and no simple statement can answer,
neither a system of logic,
followed to the last letter,
can ease the mind's chatter.

Though ultimately,
it would seem humanity
would most like
to use this opportunity

to craft a new Hades.

(Aside)
>Trust me, I been buying property-

Madonna:
Determination cannot disgrace humanity!

Who are these poor souls?
>*[She stands, gesturing.]*
I will light their way!
No beast, whether real or illusory,
is impervious to righteous gaiety.
For each and any body,
our potential rises daily,
and moreso with every act of bravery.
Surely, tis only a matter of time and pressure,
that their prayers be answered.

To you, I proffer:
to always remember,
that impossible is nothing,
but a sheep in wolf's clothing.

If I have heard correct,
as your intellect belies,
how could you deny,
a kiss, not upon the body,
but upon the mind?

We could be served even better,
with the words of a wise bartender.

Saltpeter:

> *[He chuckles, semi-charmed.]*

Such splendid candor,
a kiss of the mind!

To respond, in kind:

If the way be deliberate,
forward thought can equate to a walk,
where pacing is an important part.

One may then spy goals abroad,
above and beyond,
ceaseless intrusive thoughts.
Conversation may convert crises.
and prime potential energies.
As the wheel spun continuously,
gains greater gravity.

So, to thee, Jim, John, and Wendy,
I may say, "With every regret ye sees,
ever more pleasing shall be the finality."

Madonna:
Exactly!

Saltpeter:
Would you be so gracious
as to take a fore-handed critique?

Madonna:
Certainly.

Saltpeter:
For though, Madonna, you understand that path,
of a *spontaneous* nature, is your dance.

For those who negatively reflect,
can be aided to act,
as spoke your actions so recent.

You ask for answers
as you shower about the solution!

And I may confirm, indeed, that
these showers have produced great fruit.

All across the expanse of wide earth.
May your life-giving water
spring miracles and ever rain thirst-quenching.
    [He pauses.]
For certainly, verily,
how terrible it would be,
were fire to find victory
in that fundamental battle.
    [puffing his pipe, grinning]

What ever would we do?

Madonna:
Perhaps the better outcome
requires these forces intermingling?
   [She laughs and throws a glove at him.]

Saltpeter:
I shall certainly confirm
that your thinking is forward!
   [He chuckles.]
If I had my druthers,
I would accept your offer.
Indeed, there are few finer sports.
than a gauntlet thrown in love's court.

But all the same,
such wishes are in vain.
As you know my position
is that of 'go-between'.
My mission dictates little variation,
for with all negligence
comes great consequence,
The sentence of Sisyphus
was weak, in comparison.

Madonna:
Yes, yes, I know.

But you are such fun to play with!

[She laughs. Other folks ask for Saltpeter's attention at the bar. He obliges them.]

******

[Madonna turns to the party. Scraps and objects litter the surrounds. Seth stares into the orb. Alexander and Tonya have rejoined the party. Clarence stands in a far corner.]

Party-goer:
[to Clarence]
Hey, what are you staring at?
Come and join us.

Wait, didn't you whip out your dick?
Ha, that was some funny shit!
[to his friends]
This is the guy!

Clarence:
Oh, did you see that?

Looks like your face caught
a bit of splash-back...

Party-goer:
Bullshit, where?
[searching with his hands]

Clarence:
It's a little higher,

and to the left,
no, your left,
here...

It's right next to your naivety,
and just below the septus gullibus.
　　　　[reaching toward him, pointing]
Right about... there!
　　　　[He slaps him.]
Well, what do you know?
　　　　[The party-goer is clearly upset.]
Looks like I got it with that one.
Yep, it's gone!
　　　　[The man is not amused.]
The-the naivety...
Get it? Haha...
　　　　[Clarence laughs nervously and prepares to run.]

Party-goer:
Fucking jerkoff!
　　　　*[He charges Clarence and connects with a running
punch to the gut.]*

Clarence:
Flurverherger!
　　　　[He reels about and collapses onto the couch.]

****

Madonna:
Oh, what folly.

******

Bang!

*[The upstairs door swings open. The music shifts to
an upbeat. Proteus steps out and jogs his way down the stairs.
He gets to the landing, sees the objects and begins on them. He
empties and then disassembles a pistol in seconds. Attaches some
wires on an electric device, powering it up. He juggles some
apples successfully. He looks into the green orb for a moment or
two. A gadget of sorts materializes in his pocket. He sets it on the
table. He spins around the groups, dancing.]*

Proteus:
Sorry I'm late ya'll!

I was busy running the decathalon,
in each and every metric I could find,
refining my body and mind,
sharpening skills, talents, creations,
in actuality and in practice.

I am a man of high-genie-ology,
a spirit, evoking through a gifted body.
And thanking God for the opportunity.

I will usher in the next century, if not already.

With intellect beyond mortal fairy tale,
words, acts and monuments,
established as a matter of fact.

A habit of unique and original methods,

21st century times New Roman,
each feat detailed and described,
while balls to the wall every night,
working the human battery,
grounded and branching
out, up, and through,
an energetic pattern,
as random as Brownian motion,
yet consistent as thermodynamics.

[He slips a pair of wires from his sleeve to his hand. He snaps the air between them, and it crackles a blinking electric bolt.]

Party-goer:
Dude... what?

Proteus:
I like to ride the wavelengths.

[Proteus sleeves the wires. He sees Madonna and walks to the bar.]

Proteus:
How you doin'?

Is this spot taken?
Could an ear or a voice be lent?

Mind if not mere seat,
but a bit of your attention?

Pleased to meet your highness.

Madonna:
That's some high-minded talk
from a man playing in the sand,
drawing a seductive angle of temporary nature,
sooner washed away than to linger.

Proteus:
Tis only til they be inscribed.

Rivulets of sand pattern the beach I trace,
tested in practice, to recreate each evening's waves.
And in effect determine which to etch.

Madonna:
What I see is you're seductively sketchy,
and running your eyes all over me.
Do you see any beauty besides skin-deep?

Proteus:
My lady, rest assured,
this aspect I certainly do notice,
but there is elsewhere of focus.

For
as lovely
the look *of thee,*
tis the look *ye give,*
that dazzles me.
An aura, a beacon of energy-

Madonna:
You're doing the aura line!
> *[She laughs, then pretends serious.]*
I know you sensed that about,
even were you without the room-

Proteus:
- three hundred and sixty degrees,
across every dimension-

Madonna:
- like cosmic-rays, this enigmatic starlet
permeates the most-crowded space-

Proteus:
- tis blinding-

Madonna:
- an hydrogenous heroine
releasing fusion energy
across the spectrum,
enough light to power the creation of life.
> *[They pause.]*

Proteus:
You've convinced me.

Madonna:
See?
I like to play flattery.

Eye for an eye, eh?
Go on now, don't delay.

Proteus:
Just a few things, I have noticed.
With every word, every gesture,
every curve is immaculate,

And note the similarities.

Don't you see? You know me.
Don't deny, sure as you be beauty.
Sure as the sun shines from your day,
sure as the motion you make mine to shake,
to wave, to gyrate,
right beside an angelic,
godly creation, you...

Eye for an eye, right?

You give me yours, I give you mine.

Like a futuristic spell, it foretells
greatness awaiting our meeting.
        [he pauses]
How about a question?

Who have you been,
what, where and when?

Sure as the sun shines,
I should like to hear it.

Did events eventuate your way?

Madonna:
Perhaps I will keep those thoughts a mystery.

Better not dive beneath
when you've yet to wade the beach.

Proteus:
Yes!
    [he laughs]
Let us enjoin then,
in a toast to that end:
"To mysteries remaining mysterious."
    [they drink]

(Aside)
    Leaves a lot uncertain to have faith in.
    Still, ya gotta put it somewhere.

My lady, you are a rarity.

Madonna:
Jane may call you a suitor,
putting your neck out there.
    [she laughs]

But what if I were a hangwoman,
hell-bent on your destruction?

You know what I could do?

Dispense with all manner of tact
around your best friend,
attack your moral compass,
deny facts,
lay ruin to your relationships,
and make you think you deserve it.
    [she growls]
Then,
I would pick up the scraps,
every piece you had left,
and put you back together
like more of a gentleman.

Proteus:
I wonder what a rebuild may entail?
Might it involve strengthening romantic muscle?
    [he laughs]
I certainly don't believe it.
but fine, as ye wish,
keep it in your pocket.

I will offer the first kiss,
be it bitten or trusted,
to feel you fair woman.

Your style has gripped my smile,
and you now possess my eye.

Perhaps Odin was a prior love,
"eye for an eye", taken literally.

Formerly, however, I must warn,
I was forced to battle monsters,
and found great thrill in
the field of war and the bedchambers.

If ye aim to break,
I aim to remain.
Send your waves of gaze.

For I challenge whether
your light bends stone
as well as water.

Madonna:
Ahh, but my eye is rare treasure.
As much as you prize your own,
I prize my other.

And for whom have you thought it otherwise?
For her or them?
Or forbid it- him?
          [indicating Clarence on the couch]
I see your active wake.
It draws indeed,

right about gravity, you be,
but is that your only specialty?

You certainly have sight,
but can you feel me?
            [She rises to her feet and touches his chin.]
Could you respond in kind,
            [lightly dancing]
with a slight brush of motion,
breach the electric of the skin,
gently grip,
and press the right buttons?

Let's say,
you shook to shock my hips so,
that I was yours to sway?

Could you give your word
and the reality?

Proteus:
            [He gets up and joins her.]
Free reign at the hip,
comes with attachments.
Still, a tandem team may
dance the right direction.

Madonna:
If a direction were dreams,
mine would be a difficult variety,

hard to effect, but not impossibly.

Proteus:
Ah, the greater the challenge!

Please, allow me then,
participation in the fruition
of those dreams and aspirations.

A most intriguing journey.
it would be.
Seeking passageways
to surmount peaks,
winding way past twists and fringes
to a mountain not yet existent.

That is to say, with these hands,
your wish is my command.

For I now search to find
another's grandest fantasies,
whose finality I could furnish,
for my wishes are finished.

In fact,
the last one was just spent
upon taking your hand.

You have found a djinn,
searching for a master,

with lamp at full glow,
illuminating the night's explorations,
exuding the summation of these wishes,
now as certain as mathematical constants.

Still so much this soul to bleed,
that astronomical feats
can be achieved in this reality.

This, my lady, I would swear to thee.
With your touch... anything.

Madonna:
You... are a genie?

I've been warned about you,
promising the grandest things,
and dropping habit after the act,
once you got yourself... wet.

Proteus:
I speak not in jest,
for you enshrine the body electric.

I could not walk away,
neither now nor after the fact.
To do that is akin
to willful ignorance,
a character flaw I lack.

My greatest efforts
pale ever to your divinity.

Yet paramount would be your paradise,

Your every need, I would satisfy.

Do you like the feel of that reason?

I would raise you specifics.
given of my soul truest.

Your wishes would be reality.

Love and beauty,
a seed for tremendous tree,
growing behind the scenes,
of a concerted expression
of rapturous ecstasy.

While singing to your beauty,
this carpenter you asked for,
chief dream-crafter,
would enhance your beams,
strengthen your scaffolding-

Madonna:
    [She chuckles.]
A woodsman word-smithing a woman...
Is this a common negotiation?

My man, perhaps you could be,
but some haggling is necessary.
Tis no certainty, for to call
the pot-of-dreams, you must
play your hand visibly.

Proteus:
See here, besides you,
no other soul more capable.
And beside you, I attest.

That is my intent.
These eyes waver not,
they search and implore,
seek to explore, whether
your eyes are their home,
on a permanent journey,
joined at the pace we make.

> *[The music changes to a waltz. Proteus and Madonna
> glide about, spinning and swinging to the beat, the rhythm
> swaying, lifting, jumps, etc.]*

****

> *The party is in excellent spirits. Smiles and laughs about
> the room. Spotlight on Clarence, finishing leftover drinks from
> the table. He ruminates.*

Clarence:
(Aside)
> A couple, oh so lovely.

A couple, oh so lovely...

And so queer, this reality,
like an infinite jest on replay,
Wasted on mouth-breathing,
fume-emitting, endlessly-breeding,
sons and daughters of Babylon's bitch
that later take a joke than a dick.
[He laughs]

The best part of the jest ill-received,
tis relating precisely why that be...
[He raises his glass and addresses the crowd.]

I propose a toast!
To a couple, oh so lovely!

Crowd:
Hear, hear!
[The crowd toasts with much frivolity.]
Proteus! Madonna!
[Proteus and Madonna perform a dance move and laugh, raising their glasses.]

Clarence:
[raising his voice above the clamor]
My friends, yes!
They are a lovely pair,
who seek to live mightily.
Such a grand old couple.
May they get married

and have lots and *lots* of babies.

Yet-
and here's the rub, gents:
　　　[deliberately]
for naught he
nor she nor you
nor they understand,
that naught is underlying!
　　　[He dashes the glass to the ground.]
That abyss, deep and empty,
with senses unfit to see,
and if memory serves,
serves little consistently.
Such great uncertainty
'tween dream and reality,
to pick either foolhardy!
　　　[Grabbing someone by the shoulders]
The ground so slippery,
that slopes endlessly,
like a treadmill uphill,
constantly running!
　　　[dashing objects off the table]
There is no sense to it!
But the most interesting thing!
　　　[He gives a guy a wedgie.]
Ha! Watch the spasms,
the gyrations of him!
　　　[He swipes a bottle from someone, gulps a swig.]
On with the spirits!

Hell in a hand-bucket!

Perfect for you teeming roaches,
pretending pathetic lives,
dreaming full futility,
while death is every reward,
for misery and splendor.
It makes no matter!

Your emotions are worthless.

Your efforts are wasted.

Your revelry, an illusion!

Oh, you claim the game's worth the stake,
"Bring what pain and misery,
so long as you beside me."
        [He feigns wiping tears from his eyes]
Oh, such sweet nothings!
Share and share alike,
in shared delusion,
you cretins fawning and crowing,
all the live-long night,
Tis a calamity, told by an idiot!
That's right-
        [pointing at Madonna]
A cacophony!
Full of sound and fury!

Now-

[seeing the sword]

let's make this fury a bit more interesting...

[Clarence pulls the sword from the wall. He studies it for a moment and then swings it around wildly, hooting and hollering.]

The sword! It swings toward thee!

[people dodge the weapon]

Bystander:

Stop it! You'll kill someone with that thing!

Clarence:

Ha, you meager man!

[Clarence points it at him.]

Do you not see the plan?

Merely a placeholder, this humble "I",
who quite accidentally
wields the weapon of your demise.

I bring little prematurely,
but indicate that inevitably!

The stone shall weather away,
the sun shall boil the sea,
the sand be as glass,
and the flame finally extinguish.

And this lodging?

Short, devilish and uncertain.
With blinders upon the senses!

The mind?
Mere echoes from the abyss!
And such hollow ringing!

Your world has made a mockery of decency!
[Toying the sword at the man]
And wouldn't you know it,
you're first in line for education-
[He slices at the man's waistband, dropping his pants.]

Clarence:
I would call that prime learning. Ha!
Who else would like a proper lesson?
[He moves amongst the crowd, pointing the sword.]
Any takers?

Any heroes amongst you cowards?
[A guy starts piecing back together the pistol that
Proteus disassembled, quietly, away from the action.]

You, bartender,
say something clever.
play that devilish character.

Saltpeter:
You're insane.
And tis not my purview
to entertain.

Clarence:
Not your "purview"?

Ha! How far fallen God's chosen,
once the greatest of villains,
now a meek and humble servant,
attached to a scrap of parchment!
    [to Alexander]

And you, Mister Revolution?
Does your vague rhetoric
translate to action?
Or are you really one of
your "suburbanite children"?

Alexander:
And encourage your madness?

I know well enough
not to do such.

Clarence:
A putrid, pathetic excuse.

You got some real,
straight talk for us. don't ya?
Straight out of your ass!
    [to Tonya]
Did you see that, pithy princess?
Your lover here is little but hot air!

162

And while we're at it, mistress,
you can take all your hair-brained
academics to the grave awaiting history.
It's ultimate resting place for times infinity.
Try whipping that,
with your whack logic.

> *[Clarence comes to Proteus and Madonna.]*

Now this pair,
indeed, oh so lovely...

What you be doing, with such dancing?
Do you not know the ineffability of being?
The futile pursuit of your coilings?

Proteus:

Listen, sir,
there may be something to what you speak,
but please,
we have an eve to enjoy.
You've made your point.

> *[Proteus edges toward him]*

Give me the sword,
come on,
join the party-

Clarence:

Ha! And fall for your treachery?

> *[Clarence brandishes at him, speaking deliberately.]*

Ye've learned much from the snake,
to feign such impression.

You two like Adam and Eve,
shaking and styling with innocence,
willful cousin to ignorance.

Bleating lambs.
on the eve of destruction,
with nothing to show but indulgence!

You stand before the man
with true power in his hands,
I shall never relinquish!
For it is beyond steel,
that of inevitable reprimand!
>	*[He pushes the sword closer, jabbing at him.]*

Guy:
>	*[He cocks the hammer on the pistol and points it at Clarence.]*

Don't move! I'll shoot!

Proteus:
No, don't!

Clarence:
Ah ha! We have a winner!

Guy:
Put down the sword!

Clarence:

About time we had a match!

You bring it my friend,

and foe, you fiend!

[He jumps about, spinning, bobbing, weaving around the stage.]

I dare ya, see what happens!

Proteus:

Don't shoot! Put it down-

Clarence:

Do it!

Guy:

Bastard!

[He pulls the trigger. It clicks. Click, click, click.]

Proteus:

I put the powder in the pin-

Guy:

Oh shit...

[The gun starts to smoke and spark. He drops the gun and looks up at Clarence.]

Clarence:

You are dead!

[charging the guy]

Guy:

Oh shit!

[People clear away from him, and he's caught against the wall.]

Clarence:

Arrrgh!

Proteus:

Stop!

[Proteus leaps in at the last moment with a steel cane, blocking the sword.]

Proteus:

If ye dare to fight, fight me.

You will miss none of the fun.

[Proteus steps back, takes off his shirt, kicks off his shoes, and gets into a balanced position.]

Care to march into the storm?

Or shall I collapse your parade with a single drop of rain?

Clarence:

How now! Your arrogance knows no bounds!

[He swings at him, but Proteus deflects.]

Ah, about time we had ourselves a proper match!

It's like pulling teeth with you people!

So answer me this, you foolish snake,

whether he who holds power, holds fate?

Proteus:

As if one could ever truly

be granted such a wish,
angels and demons
would descend upon
that mockery of justice.

Be as that who wield
the sword ever to punish?

And if that be so, strike and take note!
> *[Clarence swings further, stabbing, slicing. Proteus blocks and deflects each attempt, Around the room they go.]*

Clarence:
Must be a kink in the elbow,
causes one to miss so.

Hear now, another riddle:
what use in living if temporary?
> *[Clarence comes down hard, but Proteus blocks with the cane.]*

Proteus:
All life predates your questioning!
> *[shoving Clarence backward]*
At that, only if one fancies time, a thing.

Clarence:
Hmm...
Perhaps, worthwhile it be-
> *[Clarence pauses]*
if to gut your insufferable reasoning!

[By now, the crowd has backed against the wall and barricaded themselves behind furniture. Proteus dodges and deflects heavy blows.]

Proteus:

And you scoundrel, bleeding profuse nonsense!

[Proteus hits Clarence's chest with the butt of the cane.]

Clarence:

Ah, ha ha! You have yet to see the most profuse bleeding!

You and your woman dancing,

know ye to tell dream from reality?

[He slices Proteus along the leg.]

Where is the certainty, my poor scientist?

Could you induce a conclusion for me? Huh?

Oh wait, hey, how about we have a vote!

Or better yet, let's conduct a survey!

You know nothing!

Pathetic!

[Clarence swings down hard. Proteus is on the defensive, limping slightly.]

Eyes and ears deceive!

True reality is beyond

your sad comprehension!

[Clarence advances, one swing at a time. Proteus braces himself along an upturned table, blocking with the cane.]

Mere tremors in the mind,

self-delusion, conceit!

No need for a devil-of-the-sensory,

you perceive only whims and fantasies!

> *[Clarence beats Proteus down to a knee, as Proteus uses both hands to hold back the attack.]*

And a mere nothing they be, lost to eternity!

The abyss stretches out before thee!

Thy life is forever empty!

> *[Proteus and Clarence struggle face to face behind their implements. Clarence cackles maniacally, all of his weight upon the sword upon Proteus's cane. Proteus grits his teeth, breathing heavily, visibly shaken.]*

Proteus:

(Aside)

> An abyss stretches out...
>
> Universe forever vacant...
>
> Beauty illusory...
>
> Beauty... illusory.
>
> Beauty illusory!
>
> Of course!
>
> To tell dream from reality,
>
> it is all in the telling.
>
> *[A fire alights in his eyes. Proteus gathers his strength.]*

Behold! Behold the illusion!

> *[He rises to his feet and knocks Clarence back with a strong push.]*

Does thine eye confuse truth?

[Proteus advances with strong swings.]
You rake, aloof, spurning connection!
Your brothers and sisters, in enraptured tones,
speak to your very bones!
[He connects with a kick to the chest.]
Deeper than the senses, across and between
an abyss of your own making!
[Proteus hits him with further blows.]
Memory fleeting, but only through memory thy be questioning!
As even the lowest creature asks 'what is that?',
action and truth, before doubt, do dance!

Hung up, ye be, on the mote in the eye of the gnat!
[Proteus knocks the sword out of Clarence's hands.]
If delusion were poison,
then poisoned you be!
[Proteus hooks Clarence's foot, upturns him, and catches his shirt in his fist as he falls.]

Poisoned beyond belief!
[Proteus whips Clarence on the head, knocking him senseless. He drops him to the floor.]

Ye of little faith!
[Proteus stands above Clarence, cane to chest. He straightens up, checks his wounds, and deems them minor.]

Proteus:
Now, if you will excuse me,
I shall return to dancing.
And please, take this cane,

symbolic in meaning,

as a token of our parting,

> *[He drops the cane with a clatter. Alexander, Tonya, Seth and others tie Clarence to a chair. Some begin cleaning up the great mess made.]*

Clarence:

Ughh... you... demon... visions...

****

Proteus:

> *[speaking in rhythm to the music, dancing]*

Oh enchanted evening!

What spells thee cast!

Nowhere a happier man!

Would this be a heaven, my lady?

Entwined so,

with each swing,

each swirl,

the water tightens spiral,

such priceless charms

betwixt these arms.

A party,

to your all-encompassing beauty.

We dance accused,

of letting loose truth.

Who could deny the fact of the act?

Tantamount to a level doubt

Descartes would ask-

Madonna:

     [She puts her finger to his lips.]

Shhh.

The fight is finished.

Save your tongue's twists

for pleasure in private.

For verily, as word joins ability.

     [whispering]

these lips and these hips say: yes!

     [They kiss.]

****

     The party is clearing out. People finish their drinks and exit off stage. Saltpeter is the last to go and he flips out the light. Silence. A small spotlight glimmers down on Clarence. He wakes up groggily, tied immobile to a chair.

Clarence:

Well, here we are again.

It's pitch black and you're in pain.

And... tied to a chair?

That's different.

Hey! Where'd ya'll go?

A sorry excuse for a bind.

I will be out in no time!

You hear that?

You can't hold me back!

     [He struggles with the restraints.]

This world aches with pain and misery!

Your just desserts are coming!

It is fate, it is destiny!

Inevitably, irrevocably!

I shall see to it-

> *[The chair starts to tilt.]*

Whoa...

whoa...

AHHH-

> *[Clarence falls over with a crash. He starts to chuckle, growing to heavy laughter.]*

Haha, do you see it?

The void! The abyss!

Can I get a witness?

HAHAHA!

Did you see that?

Oh this is comedy gold!

I totally told you guys!

You didn't listen, and I-

> *[He smacks his lips.]*

Mmm, tastes like whiskey....

> *[Slurp, slurp, slurp...]*

Garret C. Tufte was born in 1984 in Winona, Minnesota.
He currently resides in Lawrence, near Kansas City,
Kansas. Land surveyor by day and one of many
characters by night; he will often be found writing,
carving stone, building contraptions, or playing piano.
More of his work may be found on his website:

www.tuftesvariations.com